The Attributes of Mastery

The Attributes of Mastery

Blanca Beyar

**AYNI
BOOKS**

Winchester, UK
Washington, USA

First published by Ayni Books, 2012
Ayni Books is an imprint of John Hunt Publishing Ltd., Laurel House, Station Approach,
Alresford, Hants, SO24 9JH, UK
office1@jhpbooks.net
www.johnhuntpublishing.com
www.ayni-books.com

For distributor details and how to order please visit the 'Ordering' section on our website.

Text copyright: Blanca Beyar 2012

ISBN: 978 1 78099 453 6

A CIP catalogue record for this book is available from the British Library.

Design: Stuart Davies

Printed in the USA by Edwards Brothers Malloy

We operate a distinctive and ethical publishing philosophy in all
areas of our business, from our global network of authors to
production and worldwide distribution.

CONTENTS

The Attributes of Mastery

Acceptance

Acceptance honors the perfection in all things and in the manifestation of divine order. We may not always agree with the outcome of situations and events, however, bringing honor to all of creation, acceptance allows us to eliminate the energies of judgment and separation by accepting the collective cause and effect of every weave of creation. Acceptance unifies and honors all things.

Authenticity

Authenticity invites us to be true and naked to our resonation of spirit within the Self. No longer bounded by the opinions or judgments of others, we are free to voice our expressions and our beliefs without dishonoring the truth of others but surely, not denying our sacred Self. Authenticity is a powerful attribute that invites other to express and walk in the garb of uniqueness and freedom.

Boldness

Boldness allows us to shed away the energies of fear and limita-tions. Boldness calls for us to claim our truth and to also carry and display the mantel of divinity without fear of ridicule, of mockery or judgment. Boldness gives us the strength to move mountains and reach the highest states of enlightenment because it is truly the God Force that is in "action and movement."

Compassion

Compassion is an attribute that surpasses "feeling sorry for someone." Compassion is the quiet understanding that even amidst the painful choices and circumstances that may surround us there is always a purpose and opportunity for growth. With this realization, our hearts are always filled with love, support and light for others but it is also filled with reverence and acceptance in the enfoldment of all things without the element of judgment or separation.

Courage

Courage allows us to drop all the labels of "should or could" that are tainted with fears of being judged or ridiculed. As we transcend and allow the spark of our divinity to rise, we no longer fear the external chatter of right or wrong but trust completely in the strength that we possess to have a voice and expression in the name of Oneness. Courage is the attribute that opens the door to freedom and to wholeness.

Devotion

Devotion is an attribute that harnesses the energies of loyalty, dedication, deep love and commitment to a cause or situation...or in a master's view, to all things! Devotion is the fuel that supports all things in motion that have not yet surfaced but that are being held in the steadfast energy of trust in the heart of a master.

Evolution

Evolution is much more than growth; evolution is about expanding ourselves beyond the limitations of physicality. The evolution of mastery comes when we can embrace every experience of change, recognizing that moving forward is the only direction that can unveil an evolving soul.

Faith

Faith illustrates our steadfast belief and trust in a higher power that although it may be unseen or untouched, it is surely felt and experienced in our souls as a firm establishment of conviction and truth. It is through the practice of faith that we can "move mountains," witness the impossible and experience the joy of miracles every day and every moment of our lives.

Forgiveness

Forgiveness expresses the pureness and humbleness of divinity because the act of forgiveness can only be rendered from a place of true, unconditional love. We cannot truly forgive someone if we are tainted with emotional pain, but we can forgive someone if we are filled with eternal love and grace. Forgiveness is freeing and liberating. Forgiveness is one of the most important attributes of mastery.

Generosity

Generosity speaks of giving of ourselves unconditionally from the soul and not expecting anything in return, knowing that our greatest gift is returned by the feelings that fill our heart by the mere act of generosity. In the heart of a master, what is given is always received, for, we are all One.

Grace

Grace surpasses tolerance and temperance. Grace is the flow of subtle but continuous gratitude and bliss. It is from a state of grace that a master can overcome any challenge because he realizes that he does not need to allow himself to succumb to any frequency that disturbs the constant flow of peace and bliss.

Gratitude

Gratitude invites us be filled with the energy of "thankfulness" every moment of our lives, no matter what the circumstances. A master can always find something to be thankful for and because of this, he or she can rise above the challenging circumstances of the moment. No matter how difficult your challenge, shift your consciousness to find something to be grateful for in that moment and you will surely experience grace and peace.

Growth

Growth invites us to recognize the paradox of spiritual growth; that we are always growing and yet, we never stop growing. Our journey in this realm is to expand our growth by reaping the gifts in every molecule of experience.

Honor

Honor allows us to express respect and admiration for others, regardless of their choices or external demeanor. We may not always agree with the Outer behavior of others, but we can always honor the aspect of the God Force that is surely present in the Inner casing of every soul.

Humbleness

Humbleness allows us to be soft and maternal in every expression and action that we are undertaking, recognizing that it is with softness and tenderness that the Divine truly expresses itself. Humbleness is not a sign of weakness but truly an attribute that says, "I have no need to be or feel superior or arrogant, but I am still able to be empowering and strong."

Joy

Joy allows us to be filled with passion and happiness regardless of what is happening in the outside world. This is possible because a master of joy can see the beauty and purpose of all things and can also allow the gift of being and feeling alive to lighten any dark illusion. Joy carries a very high energy, so much frequency that this powerful attribute can literally extinguish any lower energy merely by its presence!

Observation

Observation allows us to be emotionally detached from situations and circumstances so that we can truly "see" the gifts behind every experience. Observation is a tool of mastery because from an observational stand, we can be empowered enough to execute the highest actions.

Pureness

Pureness bestows virtuous, realness and authenticity. When we practice pureness, there is a deep sense of knowingness that we are complete and whole just the way we are; there is no need to be fake or to over-inflate our image of Self because pureness allows the essence of Spirit to display itself in a most translucent way.

Perseverance

Perseverance captures the passion of spirit. It reminds us that no matter how many times we fall, we can always get up. It also reminds us that at times, many doors will close and seem to indicate failure in the quest for completing a journey or goal, but we are gently reminded that as one door closes, many more open. To "Preserve" our dreams and our passion for our purpose in life is what spirit is made of! Through the darkness and the abyss of challenges, the master who perseveres is truly an avatar.

Tolerance

Tolerance displays patience, acceptance and compassion of all things and of all people, void of any traces of separation or judgment. Tolerance also captures the essence of strength and spiritual endurance, acknowledging that there will be times when we will be tested and challenged but that the attribute of Tolerance will give us the fortitude to withstand all and still remain in a state of grace.

Trust

Trust requires steadfast focus and devotion to connecting with the Omni-presence of the Divine. Trust can only be practiced when we step outside the limited confines of physicality and

KNOW that there is a higher power that can move mountains and separate the seas. We cannot learn trust; we must harness trust through constant and intentional focus on the highest outcome of all things.

Vision

Vision is the attribute that allows us to tap into the reservoir of creation and manifestation. Like the Shaman who enters a dry field and gives thanks for the arrival of water, the visionary master always sees the completion of all that he desires and that is already in fruition, even when there is no physical evidence to support it. The master utilizes the attribute of vision to bypass limitations and to tap into the vastness of all possibilities.

Chapter 1

The Meaning of Mastery

The word "Mastery" can be intimidating because, in the world of physicality, it carries tones of displaying arrogance and ego. However in the realm of spirituality, the title of Mastery bestows a profound sense of humility, pureness, wholeness and boldness in the claiming of our authentic identity. Mastery is also in the embracement and alignment with our soul's mission and purpose.

One of the quickest ways to determine where you are vibrating right now as we explore the true meaning of "Mastery" is to focus on your feelings and reaction to the word "Mastery." Does it feel powerful or does it feel empowering? Does the word intimidate you or does it infuse you?

Mastery can be a daunting word because it represents the declaration of achieving and accomplishing the skills and experiences that qualify someone to be considered an authority figure in a certain field or vocation. It is deemed appropriate, then, to envision someone who is considered a master in his or her field to not only "walk the talk" but to also "be" the reflection of his or her mastery in everything that he or she does; to be an example of that mastery in every way.

A quick look at our history will allow us to observe many acclaimed masters in their own right. We can find experts and masters in just about every vocation and profession in every walk of life. However, as we expand our discussion into the deeper realms of spirituality, I will share with you that the message that is being presented to you today has little to do with titles or experience "under the belt" in the form of education or professional achievements. No. The message that is being presented in this book has to do with the ability for each and every one of us to become Masters in the one area that everyone—without exception—can achieve with very little training or prior experience. It is time for each and every one of us to become Masters of *Unconditional Love*.

Why is the energy of love so important and what does it have to do with mastery? Why is it so vital to become a master of Love now? The energy of love is the only energy that can dramatically and spontaneously bring change and shift to every situation and circumstance surrounding our world. The energy of love is the only remedy that can bring about healing and reconciliation to the drastic separation that exists among nations and people, causes and beliefs, and the conviction of "One that battles against "Oneness."

Mastery of Love is the call of the hour because without harnessing and embracing the energy of love in all things and in all ways, we are being very unproductive in every matter and way in which we are trying to be the causation of change and healing. It is impossible to change the world; it is literally impossible to inspire the world to change when we are not holding and vibrating on the energy of love. The greatest asset that we possess to be able to help change the world is found in "Living by Example."

Mastery encompasses many other beautiful attributes that compliment the vibration of love and these principles that support the foundation of love are also the subject of this book. In order to establish the validity of some of the principles that will be outlined in this book, we will draw from and briefly explore some beautiful examples of several Masters who have walked, transformed and helped inspire an entire creation with their mere example of "walking the talk" and demonstrating their mastery through the lives they have lived.

In exploring the examples of these walking avatars, we will truly learn and discover that it is not as important to try to change a world, as it is to be a reflection to the world of the vision that we hold for the world! The greatest contribution that we can give to humanity is to be an example of pure love and to also practice and showcase the attributes that define mastery in totality and in embodiment.

Chapter 2

Living by Example

As we take a journey in exploring the lives and examples of some of the living avatars who have touched and transformed the world, it is important to note that we may all hold dear and in reverence a unique individual or individuals that may not be widely known to the mass consciousness or through the media or mainstream. There may be a certain hero who transformed your life through his or her example and ultimately, that is what is being revealed in this chapter; it is about being an example for the world, to uphold as a reflection for everyone to experience. It is not irrelevant if your hero or heroes are not well known or spoken of in text books. If there is someone who changed your life through their example, then know that this person was merely holding a reflection of who you can become and who you already are!

When I think of the many Masters who have helped transform our world, it feels like an impossible task to name only a few when there have been so many beautiful walking angels who have contributed to our spiritual evolution and growth. I am being guided to list a few that have inspired me and then you will be invited to list and identify Masters who you feel have been instrumental in changing the world and who have contributed to your own spiritual growth.

As I look into my heart to search for a being of light that has changed the world, the first Master who enters my consciousness is the **Christ Jesus.** Although Jesus is primarily embraced and known in specific belief systems, to me he was a great Master Teacher; one that came to not only deliver many messages of truth but also to be a voice and an example to the rest of the world.. Jesus spent his entire life offering teachings of hope and helping others to heal from their fears and feelings of unworthiness. Jesus possessed great courage and spiritual strength and relied on these divine attributes to deliver his message, regardless of the ridicule and opposition that he faced throughout his entire life of service.

At the apex of his mission, he was abandoned by his closest disciples and persecuted for his beliefs and teachings, but at the end, the completion of his life's purpose went on to change the entire world and created a foundation for a belief system that whether good, bad or indifferent, surely brought about unification in large sects around the world. His demonstration of compassion and unconditional love were attributes that gave inspiration and hope to his followers and still today, Jesus is revered as a Great Master Teacher.

Moving on from one of the greatest Master Teachers that has ever lived, my heart is now filled with the Divine energy of the Mother Womb, the attributes that overflow with nourishment and nurturing of others. And as I experience the love of the Mother, another Master shows up in my consciousness, the beloved **Mother Teresa.**

Known as a passionate and very independent spiritual being, Mother Teresa was a crusader, a voice and an advocate for the poor and needy. Her unconditional love for humanity and her relentless determination to bring comfort and nourishment to others often placed Mother Teresa in seemingly compromising situations with her superiors, with Government heads and with the world at large. Still, this tiny Avatar was a powerhouse as a Divine Master of service and, thanks to her devotion to peace, for unification and her passion for charity, she began a movement that is still very prevalent in the many charities and organizations that are devoted to the care and nourishment of the needy.

A more contemporary Master who gracefully opened the doors for a new paradigm to addressing disease and disharmony in the mind, body and spirit is the one and only **Louise Hay.**

Through her own example of sharing with others her trauma-tizing and abusive experiences as a child and then confronted with cancer, Louise became the Master pioneer in teaching others that it is through the actions of forgiveness, of reconciliation and self-love that we ultimately can reach wholeness and healing.

This beloved master has demonstrated that no matter how challenging our past has been, if we acquire the divine will of Spirit, we can prevail over obstacles and become a beacon of light and service. Not only has Louise published one of the most powerful books in self-help, "You Can Heal Your Life", but she also founded one of the leading Spiritual publishing houses, Hay House, which is home to many beloved spiritual authors such as Wayne Dyer, Bernie Siegel and Alan Cohen, just to name a few. Through the attributes of perseverance and grace, this amazing master continues to inspire and help heal the world today.

Although entire volumes of books can be dedicated to honoring and celebrating masters of past and present, there is one more beloved master that I would like to honor and to use and an example; our beloved **Oprah Winfrey.** This icon to so many has been one of the greatest spiritual networkers and advocates I have ever witnessed. Oprah has truly contributed tremendous growth and healing to the world, not only through one of the most popular shows in history, but she has also unselfishly opened the door to countless messengers and given them the opportunity to shine and showcase their unique gift to the world. Oprah has demonstrated by example to the world that there truly is no room for competition or separation and she has illustrated that, no matter what our past struggles or limitations have been, if we possess the *Will* and courage to believe in ourselves, we can become a voice and example for all to experience and pursue.

There are so many other beautiful beings that come to mind when I think of masters who have helped change the world through their example:

Gandhi, Wayne Dyer, John Lennon, Yogananda, Neale Donald Walsh, The Dali Lama, Michael Jackson, John Lennon, Rumi, Amma… and the list goes on and on.

In my personal life, I also have to celebrate and honor my beautiful daughter, Brenda, who was my greatest teacher in my spiritual journey, and who encouraged me to pursue my certification in Spiritual Counseling. Thanks to her persistence, I was able to create the foundation for the purpose and mission that I fulfill today. How about you?

Who are your heroes that through their example helped inspire you to grow and heal? What attributes can you identify in your heroes that you can be inspired to harness and develop? What made/make these masters so special to you?

Please take a moment to pause here. In a journal or a special notebook, begin to identify some of the Masters that have influenced and contributed to your life. Take your time and make sure to experience the full spectrum of your feelings as you compile your list. Look to experience love, reverence, admiration, honor and respect in your soul and heart as you create your list.

There is no set number; list as many or as few masters as you need to. The important part of the exercise is to TRULY and authentically identify with the individuals who have sparked the energy of inspiration in your life. It is also important to identify the attributes that they showcase(d) that inspired you: Courage, Perseverance, Integrity, Devotion, Compassion, Faith, Passion, and of course LOVE! Once you complete this exercise you will accomplish two vital goals:

- Have a blueprint of the attributes that you YOURSELF possess; and
- Have a clearer picture of what your mastery/calling in life is.

By allowing yourself to discover and to identify with some of the heroes in your life, you will also be tapping into an aspect of your soul that is expressing itself through your admiration of others. By conducting this powerful exercise you may discover what your calling in life is by merely allowing yourself to see the resemblance to your admiration in others and your soul's purpose and calling.

The reason for this is because we are all part of the same Oneness and when we are drawn to the qualities and disposition of another, we are being attracted by the reflection in them that exists within ourselves! Yes, read this again. In truth, we cannot recognize a trait or attribute in someone unless we possess that same quality of energy within our own being.

The qualities in others are merely mirrors that are reflecting and reminding us that we hold the same energies within our souls. The glitch—if we can call it that—is that we do not always recognize our own beautiful matrix of attributes, but instead live with a yearning to be like others who we admire... even though we already "are" all that we admire in others! We simply do not recognize those divine attributes within ourselves.

Can it really be true that you and I are already all that Oprah Winfrey is? Even before we complete reading and pondering the question above, our physical mind goes into the comparison mode and immediately attempts to sabotage the divine truth that is being revealed this very moment.

The ego wastes no time in highlighting the vast success and all the accomplishments that Oprah has attained throughout her career as an advocate and messenger for the world and as you ponder the question above, your ego attempts to deflate your spirit and to say: "There is no way that you can be an aspect of Oprah!" For, if you were an aspect of her, then why is it that you are not inspiring millions around the world like she has done? If you were an aspect of Oprah, then you would not be struggling financially or trying to figure out what your soul desires to fulfill and to "be." There surely must be a glitch in this new concept and philosophy!

Chapter 3

Honor Your Uniqueness

One of the quickest ways to stifle our spiritual growth and our attainment of mastery can occur when we introduce the energy of judgment towards ourselves and choose not to honor our uniqueness. Imagine what the world would be like if we were all the same in our physical disposition and appearance, in our demeanor and our essence of being. At first glance, it may sound like a great idea if we were all beautiful inside and out and if we were all in possession of a magnetic personality, if we were all compassionate and loving, passionate and devoted, powerful and inspirational. Imagine. If this were so, there would be no need to change the world in any way because we would all be a perfect example to each other!

However, one of the most powerful attributes that we possess as a consciousness is that we are all unique and in possession of an almighty energy that compliments that uniqueness: Our Free Will. With the incredible power of our free will, we are able to express our uniqueness and add a very distinct flavor to everything that we do and all that we are. It is a cosmic paradox that even though we are all "One," we are also uniquely different from each other in our physical appearance, in our expressions and in the way we chose to manifest in this world.

The God Force did not desire to express ITSELF in the same way billions of times but it did DESIRE to express itself through certain attributes that would compliment and embrace the totality of ALL that the God Force is. Ironically, each one of us is uniquely expressing an aspect of the God Force in our expression of ourselves and the God Force is expressing ITSELF through every aspect of who we chose to be. There is no exception to this rule; The God Force energy is in everyone and so each one of us is an expression of the God Force!

The greatest inquiry that remains, then, is to ask ourselves if we are being the HIGHEST expression of the GOD FORCE as we search to define ourselves… or are we separating ourselves from the highest ideals of who the God Force is by choosing to judge ourselves and compare ourselves to others instead of seeing and embracing aspects of ourselves in all that we experience, witness and admire.

We are all mirrors and reflections to each other and yet, as a unique being, there are surely many attributes and styles of expression that only you possess and that can only be expressed by you in a way that only you can express it.

One of the glitches that exists within this realm of expression is that we seek to create a model outside of ourselves that is primarily dictated by the outside world to define what and who is deemed to be successful, accomplished and acceptable. We do not realize that in the pursuit of attempting to fit into the "norm" of society, we risk losing our uniqueness and divine gift of self-expression. The highest model for a collective and unified world exists in recognizing that we are all a reflection of each other and that these reflections that we admire from each other are already a literal part of our essence. However, as unique beings, the missing pieces of the puzzle may be hidden in being able to embrace your own unique way and style of reaching those expressions that you admire in others; to find your own way to express it in your own exclusive way!

When we put up the armory of comparison and judgment, we limit our great potential of becoming who we are intended to be. We place judgments of unworthiness, convince ourselves that we do not have enough academic preparation or personal charisma to be as successful and adored as the heroes that we so admire and desire to be like. These layers of judgments act as thick blankets of blockages that will hinder us from ever becoming and fulfilling our soul's greatest potential. It is time to stop comparing ourselves to others and to start embracing our divine uniqueness.

A beloved colleague of mine and I were having a conversation one day about the different levels of holistic healing. He was sharing with me how many times he felt hurt by the ridicule that he often experienced from friends who did not have reverence for the spiritual work that he did with individuals in "the rooms;" recovered alcoholics. As he was expressing his feelings, my friend said something very profound. He said that there were many levels of growth and healing and that each of us had a role to fulfill within the many levels of healing. He pointed out to me that his mission in life was to work with souls that were very raw and physical. He then told me that my role was to work with more evolved souls. His words were very profound because they reminded me that every level of growth was vitally important and that there would always be different needs along the path to wholeness.

Years later, my friend's words would come back to haunt me as I began to question my own role in the pyramid of growth and service. Having written several self-help books and having felt the great passion of purpose every time that I channeled one of these books, I began to question why I had not reached the level of "success" as say, Wayne Dyer or Louise Hay. To add injury to my doubts, I could not get rid of the intense yearning and calling to get out into the masses and to expand my field of service. Yet, much as I have tried, the doors to expansion have not yet arrived. In searching deeply into the spiritual work that I do with the many beautiful beings who are hungry to be of divine service, I allowed myself to accept that my work with these pillars of light is as important as being in front of a million people. For I may not have had the experience yet of reaching the masses, but perhaps one of my students is going to be the next Wayne Dyer or Louise Hay! When I allowed myself to see the importance of my work with others, I was able to see that when one of us succeeds, we all succeed.

Our roles in this experience of life are very much like the wonderful movie, "Lady in the Water," where a very unique group of souls came together in order to help one soul to complete the writing of a book that would then be read by another soul, who would in turn go on to change the world. This movie perfectly captures the importance and uniqueness of every soul and also highlights the vital importance of the collective group. Each character in the movie plays a very unique role—a role that is vitally necessary in order to fulfill the ultimate endeavor and goal that is needed for the completion of the group's mission. Here, there is no superiority or inferiority in the roles but instead, a beautifully unified honor and reverence for all that are involved.

If you have not watched this movie yet, I highly recommend that you do and if you have watched it, I suggest that after reading this chapter you watch the movie again so that you can further connect to the deeper message that is being presented to you in this book and in the movie.

We all have a role to fulfill and to play in this wonderful playground that we call life. Yes, we can get caught up in the labeling and in the judgments of comparison and unworthiness. However, one of the principles of mastery is to honor your uniqueness and to allow yourself to showcase your divine talents and gifts, knowing that you were created just the way that you were and that you possess the uniqueness that you do in order to attract, work with and assist the very select group of souls that you agreed to meet with in this realm. Perhaps there is a much larger or specific group of souls that you are intended to work with in the future but as long as you detain yourself from commencing the fulfillment of your role at some level, you may never allow yourself to reach those greater heights. Realize that your apprehension and questioning, your doubts and your fears may be preventing you from beginning the greatest role you came here to fulfill. Stop questioning your potential and stop comparing yourself to others and get busy being YOURSELF.

Chapter 4

The Contracts That We Made

The room is luminous, engulfed in a golden hued light. A great white conference table adorns the center of the golden room. As you focus your attention towards the table, you recognize yourself sitting there with someone who is familiar to you. In front of you there is a canvas that has many notations, directions and symbols. You are looking at a contract in the making. You and your companion are outlining the details of a soul contract that will take place in the future in the realm that we call earth.

There are many purposes amidst the sacred meeting that is taking place. One of the goals is to illustrate the roles that you and your companion will play in each other's lives in order to assist each other towards the greatest endeavor: the evolution of your souls. You both understand that every possible scenario and choice that you make as you configure the details of your mutual soul contract will be perfect and divine. You are both aware that the roles that you will play in each other's lives may entail the execution of certain actions that may induce emotional pain on each other. On a spiritual level, you both recognize the opportunity for growth and evolution in these experiences and lovingly agree to play your individualized roles to the best of your abilities.

We made many soul contracts before we came to earth. All of them—without exception—were geared to propel our spiritual evolution on earth. As we arrive into the realm of physicality, most of us enter into a state of "spiritual amnesia" that allows us to forget the many agreements that we made. One of the reasons why we enter into a state of forgetfulness is so that we can partake in the interchange of life experiences and allow our Free

Will to gently surface without robbing us of the many moments of spontaneous creation that will also play a part in our experience on earth. However, in time, our spirit will gently navigate us to the people and situations that will ultimately set the stage to begin to fulfill our soul's contracts. This is one reason why we are sometimes drawn to someone in particular, to a group of people or to a yearning to fulfill a goal that holds an unexplainable passion in our hearts. Our soul knows exactly what it needs to experience in order to grow and expand.

Of course, in the physical realm, we rarely if ever remember that we made the powerful contracts with other souls that were going to help us achieve the many endeavors that our soul yearned to fulfill. We don't remember because most of the time, the souls that come into our lives to help us grow spiritually are playing roles that antagonize and challenge us and that trigger many emotions within us.

We would imagine that if we agreed to make all these contracts with other souls then the enfoldment of these agreements would all be full of happy circumstances and joyous energy right? Why would we agree otherwise? It seems impossible for us to have agreed to earth with souls that would actually play the roles of betrayers or abusers in our lives. Why would we agree to such a contract? Remember, in the sight of the spiritual realm, all is perfect and every circumstance and event carries the opportunity for growth and expansion.

Is it really possible that we agreed to come into this realm and to have other souls induce emotional challenges through the actions that they would play in our lives? I will humbly invite you to explore this divine truth. For we agreed to partake in many contracts and not all of them were to spark eternal and consistent happiness in our lives; many of our soul contracts were intended to ignite the attributes of Mastery in our souls and within this invitation to find our mastery, we would first have to learn how to harness many attributes that would build our spiritual backbone.

Perhaps it may be difficult to envision and accept this revelation because to do so will require for us to accept that we have unconsciously or consciously drawn to us the many challenging and painful experiences that we have had in our lives. The measurement of these hurtful experiences can scale from mild to severe in many instances:

- Being ridiculed as a child
- Being trapped in an elevator
- Losing our best friend
- Being betrayed by our first love
- Neglected by our parents
- Being double-crossed by a co-worker
- Developing a physical condition (illness)
- Losing our home or job
- Addictions
- Physical abuse as a child or in a relationship
- Unfaithfulness by significant other
- Losing a beloved one to death

These are just a few examples of the many painful experiences that some of us encounter in our lives. Why on earth would we consciously sign up and agree to partake in these hurtful experiences? There are only two choices that we can make when asking ourselves this pivotal question.

Perhaps it is our destiny to suffer and we have no control over the circumstances of how our lives unfold. There is a powerful reason why we chose to experience these emotions—we knew they would lead us to grow and expand.

If we chose to believe that we encounter painful experiences because it is our destiny—and that there is no gain or way out of the pain, then, we immediately strip ourselves from the possibility of growing and learning from the experiences. If we choose to explore that every experience is meant to be a catalyst for the execution of one or more of the principles of mastery, then we can accelerate our growth and then begin to enter into alignment with our mastery and our soul's purpose.

It may be difficult to observe how every experience that we have is meant to bring about growth and awareness when many of the experiences that we are encountering are inflicting contrary emotions, such as challenges, fears, resentment, emotional pain, doubts, anger, jealousy, separation, spiritual weakness, confusion, and a host of other negative feelings. The reason why it is so difficult to see the opportunities of growth and reap the benefits from them is because we are not vibrating on the frequency of "mastery" but most of the time we choose to vibrate on the energy of victimization, of defensiveness and physicality.

Instead of allowing yourself to fall into a trap that will only serve to get you out of your equilibrium, step into a space to explore what are the hidden gifts of growth and development within the experiences that are challenging you...because there are always gifts!

Learn how to become the observer in every situation, regardless of whether it is past or present. Take a step back and, with your mastery's vision, take an inventory of the situations and circumstances that have plagued you in the past, or that are currently weighing on you. Observe the roles that individuals may be playing in these situations and as you do this, also take into account the list of attributes that are listed in the first chapter of this book. Look to discover which attributes the situations and individuals who are challenging you are inviting you to harness? Is a situation calling for you to display more compassion? Is the circumstance pressing you to express more grace or inner-strength? Look deeply and remove any elements of emotional reaction but instead respond to the inquiries from the state of mastery.

Completing Contracts

In many instances, some of the contracts that we made with others have already been fulfilled from a spiritual perspective; the lessons served and presented for us to grow from. However, what occurs with frequency is that we have not fully accepted and embraced the gift of growth within an experience and, instead, have now began to create a completely new obligation or contract by the choices to experience animosity, anger or resentment towards the individuals we had a contract with. When this occurs, we energetically begin to create new karma, and thus new obligations, to "fulfill the lesson learnt" in another fashion, either with the same person or with someone else. Allow me to explain further.

Let us say that two friends have a fall out and the opportunity for growth was for Soul A to be gracious and humble enough to render forgiveness to Soul B. Soul A decides to remain friends with Soul B but eventually begins to display a whirlpool of emotions that include anger, resentment and judgments towards him. If Soul A could simply enter into a state of mastery and render forgiveness, he would be free to move on with or without the friendship but still gain the point on mastering "forgiveness."

However, because Soul A allowed himself to enter into a state of physicality, the opportunity to learn how to master forgiveness has not been completed. Soul A will eventually be confronted with another opportunity to learn how to master forgiveness but the experience may not be pleasant because, in order to fulfill the mastery of forgiveness, Soul A will have to experience another emotional fall out with either Soul B or another soul that will once again challenge Soul A to gain mastery in the arena of forgiveness. Are you beginning to see why we have contracts and why we are challenged in so many ways?

No one said that mastery was easy; especially when we have

not been invited or taught to look for the gifts in every experience—especially in the most challenging of circumstances within the relationships we are attempting to maintain.

Stop. Think about this for a moment. Observe the many times in which you have been challenged by someone or something and how many times the situation continues to escalate from bad to worse or continues to repeat itself in the faces of other relationships or circumstances. If this is something that you can resonate and recognize in your life, take the stance of the observer and strive to discover which divine attributes you are being invited to practice and to master.

Why does it have to be so hard to obtain mastery, you ask? It truly does not have to be as hard as we make it for ourselves. The added challenges and heartaches develop when we become stuck in the circumstances of situations and begin to harness toxic emotional energies. When we allow our emotions to dominate, we lose sight of the opportunities for growth.

Of course it is difficult to practice being the observer and to not allow emotions to surface when we are in the midst of experiencing very challenging experiences with individuals that we deeply care about. It is hard not to experience feelings of hurt, betrayal or the host of other emotions that can develop when we are being confronted with certain scenarios that involve people and family that we trust and love and are now experiencing a letdown by their actions and words, or the lack of their actions and words.

However, the choice is simple: either we get stuck in the experience and hurt, or we can take the stance of the observer and ask ourselves what roles these individuals are playing in our lives and for what purpose? From the stance of the observer, we can take an inventory of the attributes of mastery and see what invitations these experiences are laying in front of us to master.

Our surroundings and the environment of the mass consciousness do not readily support the philosophy of becoming the observer, of rendering or practicing many of the attributes introduced in this book. The reason for this is because it has become much easier to experience separation, justification and victimization. It is easier because the mass consciousness has been taught and influenced to remain in a state of emotional paralysis.

You do not have to make this choice any longer. If you can recognize that every experience is begging you to become the observer and to reap the heights of spiritual growth, then choose now to become a master of your emotions and of your self-realization towards mastery.

Chapter 5

The Blaming Game

The master teacher, Wayne Dyer, hit a home run when he was inspired to compose his bestselling book, *No More Excuses*. The title and the contents of the book really say it all. There are simply no excuses for being emotionally or spiritually stuck, or to be unhappy and unfulfilled in our lives. Although it may sound crude to say that we have no excuses, the truth is, we simply should not have any excuses.

In order to accomplish this level of mastery, where we can move beyond the mask of excuses, we first need to allow ourselves to not only heal from the past but to also honor the reasons why we have had our experiences. Then, we also need to stop blaming other people and circumstances for our perils and feelings of unhappiness.

Becoming a master of spirituality does not require us to deny our feelings and to make believe that everything is OK when it is not. Being in alignment with our spiritual truth does not mean that we have to become martyrs of circumstances and that we must allow others to step all over us and to take it without an ounce of emotional stir or spark. What it does mean is that we should begin to honor what we are feeling and acknowledge when something is not feeling good and have the courage to look at the situation head on.

Instead of entering into the blaming mode of accusing others for our feelings of unhappiness, we must take responsibility for our own feelings and we must be willing to see what messages are being revealed that need our attention.

It is very easy to say and believe that if others in our lives would simply be more attentive, understanding, compassionate, agreeable, patient, willing to communicate, less likely to become agitated, etc. that we would be able to be more relaxed and happy. The truth is that the only thing that we can do is to express our feelings to others in an authentic way and hope that they are willing and able to listen to us. At the end, we do not have the control in changing others but, as we learned in Chapter Two, we do have the ability to impact others by the example that we are reflecting in who we are choosing to be. The only person that we can truly change is ourselves. Blaming others for our perils is simply a poor excuse because it keeps us in a state of justification. If we can blame others for our misfortunes, we can then get comfortable in the victim role. In the victim role, we fail to execute any of the attributes that can bring us to freedom from the pain of blaming and victimization.

Yet the temptation and patterns to blame are plentiful. We all have our stories and emotional scars of pain from our childhood and our past. We have all, at one time or another, experienced feelings of abandonment, neglect, betrayal, cruelty, indifference, rage and violence. Is it possible to ponder that perhaps the reason why we all can relate to these painful experiences is because hidden in the matrix of each of those moments we are being given the opportunities to grow and to implement some of the attributes of mastery?

In the previous chapter, I talked about the contracts that we agreed to partake in with all the souls that we meet with in our lives. Perhaps hidden in these contracts were agreements with certain individuals who would ignite within us very deep and raw emotions that would propel us to ignite the attributes of mastery—but before doing so, these emotions of hurt and sadness would rip through us like swords so that we could spark the fire of spirit within each of us that would help us transmute these emotions into a holy and powerful attribute of mastery and love.

Why on earth would we agree to have such contracts? Why

would we agree to endure pain, suffering and a temporary loss of our divine identity? We agreed to experience pain and suffering so that we could have the opportunity to not only have the experiences but also to learn how to unveil the opposing side of suffering and pain...to discover peace and wholeness.

We never lost our spiritual identity; we simply chose to temporarily forget that we are masters of love and aspects of the Divine. We chose to forget in order to partake in the human experience in order to filter through our souls the infinite waves of emotions that the human experience renders to us as a gift. For, as much as we may dislike to feel sad and unhappy, think of all the other blissful and wonderful emotions that we are gifted with in the human experience.

Executing the energy of blame in our lives will keep us in a state of emotional blockage and it will also stifle our spiritual growth. Most of the time, the people who we blame for our unhappiness have moved on with their lives and have absolutely no awareness of the toxic energies that we are still holding in place. This may be irritating and frustrating to know but it is a reality that we should choose to look at because in truth, we are only hurting ourselves by choosing to hold on to emotions of the past.

The master of spirituality allows himself/herself to feel the emotional pain of situations but realizes that there are ALWAYS messages of growth in these experiences. With this knowingness, the master allows the physical assimilation of heavy energies to move towards a state of reconciliation while setting into motion the activation and execution of the attributes that will assist him or her to move beyond the physical emotions to a state of spiritual growth.

Chapter 6

Stay "On." No "Off" Switch

As we continue to explore some of the principles that are fundamental to living and breathing in the role of mastery, I invite you to contemplate a subject that I often speak about with my students; a principle that can be very challenging to master. It is a principle that can be very taunting to our mastery! As masters, we should recognize that we do not have an "ON and OFF" switch that deludes us into believing and accepting that it is OK to have excessive "OFF" moments of physicality.

It is a poor excuse to claim that "we are humans" and that, as such, we are allowed to have our moments of physicality. If we choose to believe that we are humans, having a spiritual experience, then we must also choose to be aware that we may never reach the higher states of mastery that we so desperately yearn to achieve. A master realizes and acknowledges that he/she is much more than a human having a spiritual experience. A master embraces the truth that he/she is a spiritual being with infinite divine attributes and that through the power of awareness and discipline; he/she can be "ON" even when he/she is experiencing a moment of physicality.

I often like to compare the experience of having a "moment" to a speedometer in a car. Some cars only go from 0 to 30 mph while other vehicles, such as sports cars, go from 0 to 100 mph. Well, as much as we may like to admire a sports car, our spirituality should not be measured by the likes of one!

It is true that we are existing and experiencing life in a blend of spiritual and physical energies and it is also true that, because we are built to experience and express emotions, we are also subjected to the movement and cycle of emotions. However, mastery is about remembering to "be in the world but not of it." This powerful statement reminds us that we can partake in the world but we do not have to be subjected to the energies of it— especially if they are not in alignment with harmony and oneness. As mentioned earlier, this is a very challenging principle to practice when we are surrounded by a variety of energies.

The challenges are plentiful and are present in our lives every day. We can be peacefully driving in our car, listening to a meditation CD, when suddenly a car from the far left comes crossing through the lanes and cuts you off. You momentarily stop breathing and then, as you catch your breath, you begin to curse at the driver. Your blood pressure begins to rise and suddenly your entire mood is shifted from that of peace to that of rage. This is an example of going from 0 to 100 in a moment.

Of course, another choice would be to take a breath after having a "moment of frustration" and then center yourself in your divine energy. Instead of allowing the individual that cut you off to control your mood for the rest of the day, you could send them some light and compassion. You can take a moment to ponder that perhaps the individual was preoccupied with concerning thoughts and totally forgot to move lanes as his exit was approaching. Perhaps the individual is late for work and has been written up in the past and now he is desperate to make it to work on time. Or simply, you can just have compassion for the individual and then let it go.

Being "On" means that, as a master of spirituality, you are conscious that your thoughts, expressions and actions are energies in motion that literally have an impact on people and situations. Being conscious of this truth, a master is discerning with his expressions and practices reverence for the power of the "Word." A master recognizes that he/she can induce instant healing or injury by the very next utterance of words that he or she expresses. The master also realizes that his/her actions have a direct cause and effect on every situation that he/she partakes in.

With this knowledge, the master strives to act from a place of love, from a place of compassion, from a state of unity and from a state of grace.

If we are truly to be an example for others to follow we must take responsibility for the production of energy that we are demonstrating and feeding into the world. Yes, we will all have moments, and yes, we will all have the choice to go from 0 to 100 or to simply go from 0 to 30 and then remind ourselves to find our balance as soon as possible. As masters, we seek to find our balance because we are in awareness that being "Off" is not a choice.

Whenever we find ourselves challenged by a multitude of experiences on a given day, we should take the time to see if we are being invited to align ourselves with the fundamental principles of mastery. Perhaps, without realizing it, we have allowed ourselves to temporarily enter into a state of "off." By taking a few moments to review the attributes of mastery, we may immediately see that we were not practicing compassion or grace in a given situation and that our challenging day may simply be reminding us that we entered into a "off" frequency. The simple act of having the awareness and of taking a moment to take inventory may be all that you need to do in order to bring yourself back to "On."

Symptoms of irritability and frustration may also be a signal that we are neglecting ourselves from spiritual nourishment. Remember that in order to maintain our spirit in the "On" position, we need to make the time to refuel our soul. If we spend too much time away from the practices that nurtures our spirit, we will surely begin to experience the feelings of depletion.

Have you identified what practices nourish your soul? Here are some helpful suggestions:

- Meditation and prayer; quiet contemplation
- Mindful breathing and releasing of emotional toxicity

- Time for relaxation and self-nourishing
- Laughter, laughter, laughter
- Walks in nature
- Healings, massages, yoga
- Creativity flow and creative activities
- Expression of love
- Smiling
- Identifying goals, feeding intentions
- Detoxifying from emotional debris
- Reading a good spiritual book

There are many ways in which we can refuel our spirit to insure that we are always "full and On." Make sure to take the time to refuel yourself and you will be taking a huge step towards preventing the onset of going on "Off" mode for extended periods of time.

Chapter 7

Stay Focused or Be Distracted

Mastery requires of us to remain diligent on our focus of what is truly important in order for us to optimally fulfill our missions in life. Staying focused is not always an easy task to practice because the world can be filled with constant distractions. In order to be steadfast in our focus of what is truly important, the master must learn how to be discerning and mindful of how he manages his time and his energy.

We can see examples of this philosophy when we explore the beautiful writings of Tao Masters. In many beautiful parables, we learn how the disciples would come to the master with quenching inquiries about life. Anxious to receive mentoring from a Master, the disciples were instead sent to rake the leaves or to dig a hole in the soil in order to "receive the insight that they needed." In other words, the Master would spend as little time as possible mentoring the disciple, knowing and trusting that the true answers to the disciple's question already resided within.

Being discerning does not mean that we should shun people from our lives and not offer them guidance and support when they are in need of it. No. However, discernment calls for the master to realize that in order for others to grow and develop spiritually, they must learn to tap into the reservoir of Knowingness within. In allowing others to become dependent on your constant guidance and support, it may actually stifle their growth and distract you from your own growth and development.

Distractions can surface in many forms and can wear many disguises. How often do you plan on taking some quality time for yourself in order to replenish and restore when suddenly a thousand things show up to disturb your quality time? Often the distractions come in the form of S.O.S. from others in the form of phone calls, emails, etc. It is important to recognize that as spiritual beings who are living to be of service, we may find it conflicting to monitor our time in helping and guiding others because we often feel that this is the "right thing to do." However, as I always say to my beloved ones, "We cannot give what we do not have."

Mastery is not about being a martyr or about compromising your own stability and wellness at the expense of helping others. Mastery is about maintaining a beautiful balance for giving but also in making the time for receiving, for Self-restoration and replenishing.

For many of us, one of the hardest words to say is "No." We often feel that we are disappointing and letting people down when we say NO to an invitation to participate in something, to be available or to make the time to connect with others when we simply cannot afford to be distracted from something that truly requires our attention.

The consequences of being unable to be discerning with your time and energy will surely be reflected in your ability to accomplish many of the goals that you desire to achieve. The added stress and frustration of feeling overwhelmed and pulled in many directions will only perpetuate your feelings of overload.

We are also challenged in many ways from achieving a steady flow of focus towards our most important goals because we succumb to the belief that we simply do not have enough time in the day to accomplish everything that needs our attention. We often sacrifice our own needs in order to accommodate other activities and obligations that have to do with everyone else but ourselves.

Oftentimes the consequences of these choices leave us to deal with feelings of resentment, of frustration and anger. What may follow are feelings of being taken advantage of; of not feeling appreciated for all your efforts and a deep feeling of being overwhelmed. Since we have gotten everyone used to have us playing the role of rescuer, we may find it difficult to get others to recognize that we also need emotional support.

In order to get the help we need we must be willing to voice and express our needs to those closest to us. A master recognizes that he or she does nothing on their own; that we all need the support of others in order to achieve any goal in life. Honoring your needs and having the courage and boldness to voice them is what mastery is all about.

Take a moment to make a list of the goals that you wish to accomplish within the next three months. Once you have completed the list, identify what you require in order to achieve these goals or the obstacles that might stop you or slow you down. Is it more time that you need? Do you need more support? Help? Guidance? Silence? Money? What?

Once you have identified your needs, think of ways in which you can meet them. Do you need to ask for help? Do you need to unload some responsibilities or obligations? Do you need to make changes in your life? Do you need to rely on and trust others more? Do you need to let go of some things, people, beliefs, limitations, excuses, fears? As you work on your list, also explore what kind of changes and modifications you can make in your schedule and lifestyle that will assist you in remaining focused on the more important things in your life.

There is a reason why the word "distraction" rhymes with the word "extraction." Distractions extract precious energy from us and leave us feeling depleted, exhausted, helpless and frustrated. Learn how to conquer your distractions by committing yourself to identifying and eliminating situations and obligations that do not serve your template towards mastery. Commit yourself to remaining focused on the important issues and tasks that will heightened and support your spiritual growth and seeds of intention.

Chapter 8

Be the Master, Not the Preacher

In chapter 2 we learned about the beautiful art of living by example and I share some amazing stories of masters who have changed the world by "walking the talk" and by breathing and living by the attributes of mastery. When we are living by example there is no need for labels, titles or for external recognition because we are fueled by the vibration of our unique, divine spirit that is in alignment with pureness and humbleness.

Because we are harnessing authenticity and also recognizing the Oneness that exists within all of us, there is no need to display arrogance or superiority in our expression of Self or in whatever position of service we are fulfilling. We are able to "simply be." However, at times, when we are not diligent in observing and in practicing the attributes of mastery, which include humbleness and tolerance, we may find ourselves tempted by the ego. If this occurs we may begin to vibrate in a state that I refer to as the "Preacher Syndrome."

The Preacher Syndrome often masks itself as seemingly innocent and concerning in nature. The "Preacher" may spend unnecessary amounts of time and energy concerning himself with the choices that others make and also may obsessively devote time to highlighting the consequences that may develop in the lives of other people. In an unconscious way, the Preacher may be in breach of breaking the principle of non-judgment towards others.

The Preacher will usually take a stance that he or she is simply noticing the "flaws" in others out of concern, when what is really occurring is that the ego is taking a stance in the energy of arrogance. The Preacher who practices arrogance may also in breach of practicing humbleness and honor for the journey that others may need to undertake in order to grow from their choices through experiences.

There can be hidden messages and signals in individuals who constantly need to preach and who have a need to be constantly engaged in discussing others who are not as spiritual as they are. The Preacher Syndrome can become a masked escape to judge others, to deliver a sense of superiority and to help avoid looking at the Self in a deeper way.

Whenever I am in session with one of my beloved students, I always remind them that they should only contemplate and explore any insight that I provide for them "if it resonates." I tell them that if it does not resonate, to kindly leave it at the door. In other words, my job as a guru is not to preach, to impose my truth on them or to act from a place of arrogance. My job is to gently guide and spark in them the inner-truth that is always within them. This gentle reminder can be done from a place of love and humbleness without the need for superiority or arrogance.

I also share with my students that they are my greatest teachers. For there have been many, many times when I have been reminded of an attribute of mastery and lifted from a dark moment just by spending some time with one of my beloved ones. I am constantly reminded through their devotion and efforts to heal and to ascend of just how much they have grown, and that in turn fills me with joy, gratitude, purpose and love.

We are constantly mirrors and reflections to each other. Whether we realize it or not, we are always projecting and reflecting our energy and our emotions through the vehicle of how we are choosing to be from moment to moment.

The greatest way that we can help others is to be the example of a master in motion, in expression and action. This is the greatest tool that we have to assist others in shifting their vibrations.

There is no need to preach or to feel obligated to teach others what we have discovered in our own spiritual journey and development. Yes, you can share and inspire. You can humbly recommend a good book or share a spiritual philosophy that worked for you but, at the end, simply honor and allow others to grow through their own experiences.

Oftentimes the "Preacher Syndrome" can be seen in initiates who have recently begun a spiritual path. So eager at discovering the principles and philosophies that can lead to wholeness and freedom, initiates immediately step into the mode of preachers, trying to impose what they are learning onto others. I gently but always remind them that knowledge alone does not make someone a master, but truly practicing and breathing the principles to the best of our ability is the surest rode to mastery.

One of the quickest ways we can discover if we are unconsciously vibrating in the energy of the Preacher Syndrome is by observing your responses to others. Are you experiencing exasperation, frustration, anger or intolerance when others do not follow your advice? Do you feel insulted or agitated when others are not listening to your suggestions? Do you feel preoccupied by other people's lives? If you have answered YES to any of the questions listed above, you should take inventory of your ego and start learning how to become more of the observer.

As much as we would like to help and see others that we care for commence a healing path, we should be mindful to remember that we cannot impose our truth on anyone. We should also be aware that experiencing excessive amounts of frustration or intolerance towards others simply because they are not willing or ready to change is a masked energy of arrogance. It is OK to have moments of sadness or frustrations because those that we love are not choosing to heal, but at the end, we must recognize that our choice to heal came from our own inner-state of readiness and willingness.

Chapter 9

Are We Humans or Spiritual Beings?

This may sound like a silly question when we take into account that we are discussing the attributes that lead to "Mastery"! Are we merely humans attempting to become Masters in a very challenging physical realm? Or, are we really spiritual beings— Masters—allowing ourselves and partaking in one of the most amazing experiences... the human experience?

Although most of this book is a channeling; insights that are being presented to me by the Divine Force, once in a while I am allowed to step in and contribute to a chapter. Perhaps it is my own perception that I am being allowed to speak and it is merely the God Aspect in me that is contributing!

In any event, what I would like to share is that this chapter was inspired by a beloved student who is an ascended Master in her own right. I have had the honor to work with her for several years now and have witnessed her conquer many physical and emotional challenges. I have witnessed her blossom into a beautiful master of divine service for humanity.

Recently I asked her to conduct a little "clean-up" work in order to help her release some minor residue that had been surfacing in her emotions. The emotions centered on past choices, fears and guilt of having made wrong choices. She conducted a pardon letter to herself in order to release and forgive these held emotions and as she did, she mentioned a few times that "she was only human" and that because of this, she had to forgive herself for making mistakes. As I reviewed the pardon letter this particular statement jumped out at me and I knew I had to invite my student to share in a discussion of this belief with me.

While there is never a "right or wrong" in what we choose to believe in, our beliefs can be very limiting and can literally stifle our growth... no matter how hard we may be trying to heal and grow in other ways. This is the power of beliefs. Beliefs are a vital aspect of our foundation. It does not matter if our held beliefs are positive or negative; the end result is that our beliefs will greatly contribute to our foundation. So if our beliefs are limiting and negative, our foundation will be surrounded with instability that will often threaten us with fear and doubts. A foundation formed on negative beliefs can be very crippling and unsupportive, to say the least. In order to have a firm foundation that will carry and support us, we must create our foundation with powerful and supportive energy.

Believing that we are merely humans is a very limiting belief because the human composite of our makeup is always going to experience its limitations: age, decay, wear and tear, environment, genetic makeup and death. How sad it must be to experience a life without having the knowingness of how unlimited and powerful we really are!

Being in a physical body was meant to be one of the greatest gifts of our *Spiritual Experience.* Our greatest endeavor and goal is to move through the human experience and to have the realization that we are so much more than the human composite. We can accomplish this by removing the limiting beliefs that we are only the body, which is vulnerable to the physical laws of decay and death. We are so much more than this. Our potential to experience and discover how incredible and divine we truly are primarily depends on our ability to drop the belief that we are merely flesh.

It is true that we are in a body and that as such, we are responsible for the recognition that the body has certain requirements for nourishment and maintenance. We know that in order to keep the body healthy, we should nourish ourselves with food, drink plenty of water, exercise, make time for relaxation and fun, and also time for rest. We know that the body is susceptible to vulnerabilities and to illnesses and decay. The media does a great job of reminding us of the body's vulnerabilities through the countless commercials for medications, for weight loss, for libido, and for a host of other "flaws" that can be remedied through cosmetic and physical repairs and maintenance.

Little attention is ever given—if at all—to the other aspects of our being. It is no wonder that as a society we believe that we are humans and mere mortals. The media and the mainstream give very little credence to our spiritual aspect and offer little if any guidance on how to maintain our spiritual essence. Spiritual guidance and protocol is still considered to be a religious subject and, in many cases, it is still also considered taboo. It is time for the world to reconsider its position on the importance of Spirituality and to begin to open the doors to expanded discussions, programs and media coverage on the importance of spiritual health and the benefits of how it can promote the quality of living. Our emotions play a huge part in our spiritual wellness. Our beliefs also play a huge factor. Our belief that we are limited literally perpetuates our experiences to be constricting and confining.

If we focus primarily on the body structure and give little attention to our spiritual essence, we are literally choosing to live and experience only HALF of our lives. It is comparable to walking around with half of an existence. And when we primarily focus on the perils of aging and of disease, we leave little room for the miraculous to occur in our lives. When we introduce the energy of spirituality to our lives, many situations and circumstances in our lives take an amazing transformation.

I have personally worked with countless individuals who have healed from diseases and who have also conquered many emotional and mental limitations by merely implementing and practicing a regimen of healing and spirituality in their lives. Many of these miraculous healings would have never been possible if these individuals had limited themselves to only observing and embracing their physical aspect. It was through their expansion of embracing their spiritual essence that they were able to break through the chains of limitations and unveil healing in their lives.

In order to expand beyond the confines of limitations, we must tap into the reservoir of our spirituality and explore the truth that we are not human beings having a spiritual experience, but truly, spiritual beings, partaking in the experience of humanness. It is when we align ourselves with this truth that we will finally be able to break free from the narrow-minded limitations that we have created as a society and begin to expand our consciousness, our experiences and our mastery into a whole new paradigm.

Chapter 10

Be Gentle With Self

One of the most difficult conflicts that a master must defeat is found in the constant battle that lives within the lower self in the areas of self-criticism and self-judgment. It is true that we can be our greatest enemy or that we can be our greatest force.

Through the chains of conditioning and mainstream influences, we have learned as a society to deem it perfectly acceptable to put ourselves under the microscope of scrutiny and constant belittling of our self-worth and self-value. Many of us believe that this kind of abusive treatment of the Self is necessary in order to identify our "weaknesses and flaws." There is no greater pain to Spirit than self-condemnation.

Mastery is not about being flawless and perfect all of the time. When we have mastered being in a state of perfection 24/7, trust me, we will be out of here. The Human Experience is a field of imperfection but it also offers us the grand opportunity to discover what perfection is. In other words, the Human Experience is much like Kindergarten, where we first learn the ABCs of life but we also are given the opportunity to have fun and to become part of a collective group.

Comparing the Human Experience to Kindergarten may seem unrealistic when we think of all the responsibilities and challenges that we experience in life. And yet, when we allow ourselves to accept that life does not have to be so complicated, we will then allow ourselves to have some fun in the process of experiencing.

Do you remember when you were in Kindergarten or Preschool? Perhaps some of you, like me, did not have the opportunity to participate in this kind of setting. In Kindergarten and

Preschool, most children learn how to:

- Share with others
- Discover their Self worth
- Sit and listen
- Learn discipline
- Participate in group activities
- Learn fundamental rules and practices
- Engage in new and fun activities
- Play and have fun
- Rest and have quiet time
- Learn to have a voice
- Embrace their unique identity
- Prepare for the learning years ahead

Experiencing life in Kindergarten does not have to be forever as long as we learn how to master and to also have reverence and acknowledgement for the things we have learned. However, as long as we keep ourselves under the microscope of criticism, of self-punishment and judgment, we will not be able to advance to the other "Levels" of life and mastery. Just like in school, where we must repeat a grade if we have not demonstrated mastery over certain subjects, our spirituality will keep us in the same level of ascension until we have mastered the areas of life that will allow us to move forward.

I often am asked by students if there are certain protocols that must be met in order to reach a level of mastery. I always respond the same way to this question… the greatest protocol is willingness to expand. As long as we are willing to grow and also willing to recognize that we will have to fall along the way to growth—many times—and as long as we are willing to realize that every fall is a necessary step along the way to mastery—and are willing to forgive ourselves for our judgments of failure and remain steadfast in our commitment to grow—then we will ascend and reach mastery!

Many on the spiritual path believe that in order to demon-strate their spiritual growth and strive for attainment of mastery they must adhere to a radical shift in all of their behaviors, beliefs and patterns. Many students place an enormous amount of pressure on themselves; wanting to master every attribute as quickly as possible. While I will always hold a field for mirac-ulous transformations that can happen in a moment, most often our spiritual path towards mastery is a lifelong experience... because in truth, we truly never stop growing. Mastery is a process, a journey and an arrival, moment by moment, all at once.

For many, the road to spiritual mastery may invite them to become conscious of their diets; many individuals feel a closer attunement to nature and Mother Earth when they become vegetarians or vegans. For others, the calling may be to align themselves with a particular religious sect or to practice specific rituals such as meditations and prayers. Others find peace in wearing certain garbs or totem pieces as a way of feeling in alignment with Spirit. The display of tattoos and sacred symbols holds reverence for some. Other individuals take on the name of a deity as a way of creating an alignment with an ascended master or avatar. And still, some simply decide to live a simple life as a spiritual being, having a human experience!

The point is there is truly no wrong or right way to practice spirituality or to attain mastery. If there is a calling or yearning to incorporate certain practices and rituals, by all means, if they resonate with your soul and brings you into a greater state of spiritual union, honor your yearning. Do not compare the practices that support your spirituality with the mainstream. Simply honor your Self.

Do We need a Mentor, Teacher or Guru

Throughout our lives we encounter a multitude of mentors and teachers that contribute to our emotional, mental and spiritual growth. From the day we are born, we begin our journey of learning through sounds, sights and vibrations. Our physical parents become the first line of mentors and teachers who instill in us a central foundation of beliefs and patterns of behavior. Our siblings, family and friends all play a vital part in our growth. Through our contracts, we give each other the greatest opportunities for expansion and self-realization.

As we mature, other influences such as education, politics, religion and the dominance of the media begin to also play a role in the matrix of who we allow ourselves to become, either consciously or subconsciously. Whether we are learning positive or negative things, the point is that we draw much insight and knowledge from these channels and in some fashion they are mentoring and teaching us.

There was a time when the word "Guru" was a holy title that was primarily used to define a teacher or mentor who was devoted to teaching spirituality. Today, the title of Guru has become a trendy word to describe an expert in a specific field or trade. These days, there are Food Gurus, Fashion Gurus, Internet Gurus, just to name a few. In spirituality, however, the name Guru is still observed with reverence and honor.

Our greatest Guru is the aspect of ourselves that is untainted by the experiences of physicality and powerfully filled with the pure essence of the God Force. There is a Guru in each one of us: that aspect of ourselves that yearns for Oneness and happiness in all areas of our lives and also for the world.

The Guru within can be reached and revealed once we are able to move past the veils of physicality and the gripping emotions that separate us from our mastery. The greatest way that we can tap into our Guru Self is when we begin to incorporate and breathe within the attributes that define mastery.

Perhaps this endeavor may not be so easy at first. We will need to be willing and devoted to unveiling our mastery and we must also be dedicated to becoming the observer and learn how to be conscious and aware of our movements, in thought, in expression and action in our lives.

As you embark on your journey towards mastery, you may be guided to seek a Guru to help you along the way. If you ask the God Force for assistance on your quest towards mastery, you will be guided to find a Guru who will assist you. You will know that you have found your Guru when you can see the reflection of unconditional love in his or her eyes and the spark in their eyes lights up your heart. You will also know that you have found your teacher when he or she can hold your *Divine Reflection* of Divinity for you and reflect it back to you until you can hold it for yourself; when you are ready to claim your mastery.

Finally, you will know that you have found your Guru when you can be naked in your true self in front of him or her and not feel judged, inferior, ridiculed or disciplined in a non-loving way. There is no one being on earth that is completely perfect all of the time, but you will recognize a Guru when he or she is practicing to the best of his or her abilities the attributes of mastery and, of course, of Unconditional Love.

Chapter 11

Don't Wait Another Moment... Be the Master Now!

For years now, I have been experiencing this reoccurring feeling; a sensation of sorts that has been very difficult to explain in words. Every time I would have the feeling come over me, I was convinced that I would be able to capture it and then be able to share it in words in my books and with my students but then I would not be able to... until now.

I would often find myself waking up in the middle of the night pondering the question, "What is life all about?" I would also constantly have the awareness that no matter how much we accomplished or how much we experienced, the moments would surely pass and then we will find ourselves working towards the next moment, the next experience.

In many ways this feeling that I was experiencing reminded me of the movie, "Groundhog Day," where the actor keeps waking up and experiencing the same day over and over again... but hidden in the repetition of his experiences were messages for him to make other choices that would ultimately change the reoccurring experience.

What I am about to share is my own observation of life and it surely does not have to become your truth if it does not resonate. Life is happening every moment of every day! Life is what we are doing when we think that we are not doing anything! Life is every experience, pleasant or unpleasant. Life simply is.

What we make out of life is up to us. No matter what is going on in the world, you can still experience another spectrum of life if you choose to. Life is happening! Don't wait another moment for something to happen or not happen in order to become a master of life!

Do you get it? It took me many years to understand that life is what is occurring every moment. We do not have to get to a specific place, reach a specific age, accomplish particular goals, or achieve certain things in order to live our lives as fully as we can. We need to capture every moment and every molecule of every experience and recognize that it is a part of our divine puzzle... all of it, with no exceptions.

This is not to say that we should not set goals and intentions for ourselves or that we should not work at reaching our highest potential simply because life is happening. That is the whole point... Life is happening... so, what are you waiting for?

Even if we have dedicated ourselves to learning the principles of spirituality and working on healing and recreating ourselves, we still have little pockets of expectations that will lead us to believe that we must reach or achieve certain goals in order to feel "accomplished" to arrive at the climax of mastery.

The truth is that we are reaching and achieving mastery every day by the mere act of experiencing life. There is no pedestal to reach or no mountain to climb that will confirm that you have finally reached mastery. The graduation day of mastery actually occurs when we complete our mission on earth and move on to the next realm of experience and growth.

This does not mean that you cannot attain or strive to "Be" a master while on earth. Mastery is the reason why you and I are here! Do you see the paradox in this truth? This is why it took me so many years to understand it, much less share it with you today. It is a paradox because what we are working to achieve is already achieved within the core of our soul.

We are already masters of our lives and also divine aspects of the Divine. We are simply recalling that truth and how we are doing that is by having all the experiences that we are having every moment that we are living. We will continue to move higher and higher towards mastery as we continue to experience life as we practice the attributes of mastery. We will reach a higher attainment into mastery as we achieve and manifest in our lives through experiences.

In truth, our experiences are our greatest teachers and are the steps that will lead us to ultimate freedom, bliss and Oneness. So with this knowingness, honor and embrace all of your experiences. No longer be afraid to savor and discover what the next chapter of life has to present to you. Arm yourself with the attributes of mastery and begin to practice them as you move on from one soul contract to the next. If you currently find yourself stuck in a soul contract and it is conflicting and causing turmoil, refer back to the attributes and ask yourself what is it that you need to put into practice in the form of higher, divine energy.

Remember, nothing will solve itself by itself. In order to bring fluidity and progression into a situation, there must be movement, change and, above all, there also must be growth. Don't waste another moment! Introduce a shift by practicing the attributes of mastery and you will surely witness a movement— a change—a positive change in every situation.

We are all aware that life is precious but most of us allow ourselves to fall into stagnated bubbles of experiences and we do not realize that, in doing so, we are wasting precious time. True, every moment is a moment of divine timing and, since every moment is an opportunity for growth, there really is no time wasted. However, if we are ready to move beyond the feelings of being stuck and stifled, then do not waste another moment and get busy practicing the attributes of mastery.

It is all about Love

What did the Master Jesus really mean when he said, "Love your enemies"? Did he mean that we should love those who afflict us? Did he mean that we should love those that we despise? Or did he really mean "Love everyone, all the time, no matter what"?

Did you notice that Love is not included in the list of

attributes? Are you wondering why it was not included if it is so important to practice love? Love was not included in the list because it is much more than an attribute; Love is the very essence of what we are composed of. The energy of love is what allows us to not only experience life; it also allows us to pursue our soul's mastery. The energy of Love opens the door for us to serve as masters of service for the world through our mission and purpose. It is the energy of love that drives us to the attributes of mastery in order for us to experience the essence of wholeness and bliss and then allow us to share it with others.

Think about it for a moment. It would be very difficult to practice compassion or gratitude if the energy of love was not already ignited within us. It would be difficult because the first protocol that is necessary in order to harness the attributes of spiritual mastery is to have an open and flowing heart that is full of love. Can you see the beauty of completion between the attributes and the energy of love?

Yes. The more love energy that you can hold in your heart, the easier it will be to harness and hold the energies for the attributes of mastery. And the more you incorporate the attributes of mastery in your life, the more love you will feel in your heart. It is that simple.

Yet, loving everyone and everything is not an easy task. It is an impossible task if we are still holding certain energies in place such as: judgments, separation, indifference, resentment, jealousy, anger, hatred, superiority and arrogance towards others. In order to succeed in holding love in our hearts for all things and for all people, we must first acknowledge and embrace the Oneness in all things, and this includes the good and the not so good things that manifest in the world. The reason why it is so vitally important to accept and embrace all things is because whenever we introduce the energy of judgment towards someone or something, we are creating an immediate separation within ourselves and the "something or someone." Once the energy of separation exists, it is very hard to harness any of the attributes in totality.

Acceptance and embracement of all things does not mean that we are approving and celebrating the disharmonious events that are taking place around the world; it does not mean that we celebrate wars and violence, cruelty or murder. What it does mean is that we allow ourselves to enter into a state of honoring, observing and accepting that all these circumstances that exist in our world are all here to ignite all parties involved to rise above the energies of separation and to enter into a state of Oneness and love.

We may say that this is indeed a very difficult task to accomplish when we are witnessing so much pain in the world. And yet, stepping into a state of justification and vibrating in a state of disconnection and separation will only fuel and feed the existing fields of disharmony with even more fuel of separation! Remember, justification is only an excuse to step out of the field of mastery. The attribute of observation calls for us to be detached from all situations and to become the witness of all that is transpiring. For, all that is occurring is an invitation for transformation and for healing.

Love has no boundaries or barriers. Love has no exceptions or limitations. The energy of Love is what sustains this existence in place because no matter how much we feed opposing energies, as a collective humanity, we all experience and express love, whether consciously or subconsciously. No matter how disturbed our lives may be or the world around us, there is not one day that goes by that we do not experience and express love! It must be so, for, this is the true essence of what we are made of.

In the end, we would be wise to consider that many of the disharmonious events that are taking place around the world are most likely soul contracts that were formed amongst large groups of souls, who collectively agreed to partake in these circumstances in order to spark a greater sense of collective growth and healing in the mass consciousness. Again, this does not mean that we should simply stand back and not care about what is going on in the world because it is merely soul contracts being fulfilled. No. If it is affecting the whole world and it is affecting you, then, at some level you are part of that collective group of souls and your contribution is going to make a difference, no matter how small you think it may be.

The greatest contribution that we can make towards the manifestations in the world is to surround them with the potent energies of love and of light. When this action is done, we are assisting the collective to heal from the illusions of separation and to reap the gifts of every experience, so that growth and expansion can then take place.

Love on the level of mastery has no exclusions. In order to master the energy of love, we must allow ourselves to unconditionally love:

- Those who have hurt us
- Those who have abandoned us
- Those who betrayed us
- Those who have manipulated us
- Those who have accused us
- Those who have challenged us
- Those who have turned on us
- Those who have not loved us

And we must also unconditionally love:

- Those who have hurt others
- Those who have abandoned others
- Those who have betrayed others
- Those who have manipulated others
- Those who have accused others
- Those who have turned on others

- Those who have not LOVED others

It is so because we will never truly know if these individuals were/are playing a very specific role in our lives or in the lives of others that is geared to motivate and to spark the essence of spirit within through their very actions and deeds.

We will never truly know if we did indeed sit with one another in a board room in the cosmos and eagerly agreed to be hurt and abandoned by a soul so that the experience could spark in us the attribute of perseverance and of compassion. It may sound crazy from a physical perspective but it is most likely what did occur in the cosmos as we signed up to come here to partake in this life experience!

So, in a nutshell, love it all. Be love. Be the example of love. Love all of your experiences and as you do, your unconditional loves will carry you to create and recreate new experiences that will bring you higher and higher into your spiritual mastery!

Let us remember the powerful words of John Lennon, "Life is what happens to us when we are making plans".

How Do I know?

I am often asked how I came to "know" all the things that I teach and write about in my books. I humbly but boldly share that most of the books I have written have been dictations that I have received from the God Force. I say this because after writing a book, I sit and review some of the words that I have written and I am awestruck by the divine messages and the energy of empowerment behind them.

On a few occasions, I have found myself debating with the divine presence that is guiding me to write a book; I try to negotiate with the presence; I say, "The readers may not understand this, or that is too deep, etc." Thankfully, I eventually get out of the way and allow the God Force to express itself in authenticity with the messages it wishes to deliver.

Sometimes, like right now, I am surprised by the God Force and am asked to share my personal thoughts and feelings about a subject matter that is being discussed in one of my books. As I was completing the previous chapter of this book, I was invited by the God Force to include a final chapter, entitled, "How Do I know?

As usual, I began to protest with the God Force and asked, "Why does it have to be titled in this fashion?" I felt that the title held a streak of arrogance. Then the God Force gave me a spiritual slap and reminded me of the many countless times I have used one of my own experiences in life as an example to help a beloved reach a higher state of clarity, of understanding and acceptance. I was reminded of how many times my beloved ones have received a huge gift of transformation by the mere sharing of one of my experiences.

The sharing of my experiences has had such a positive impact on many of my students because in exposing my own perils and challenges, it helps them to realize that even a guru must undergo the initiations of learning, of healing and of spiritual growth. For, as much as we would like to believe that certain individuals are born with a spiritual gift or calling, it by no means bypasses the need for the soul to reap the many gifts of growth through challenges and experiences. With this said, I truly believe that my life and experiences were divinely orchestrated not only for my own growth, but also with the intention of having me share some of the experiences as a means to spark inspiration and strength in others.

It is incredibly amazing how the God Force works! When I began to channel this book, I had absolutely no idea that I would be invited to nakedly share some of my most challenging experiences in life. I had no idea how detailed the God Force would ask me to become. I questioned and pondered deeply over the request and I also protested. I was not sure that I wanted to share some of these painful moments with readers.

But the God Force gently reminded me that it was these experiences in my life that truly served me to grow spiritually, to heal and reconcile. It was these challenges that assisted me to become a guru, the author and master of my spirituality. With this reminder, I surrendered and saw the gift in the invitation… May these experiences help you to heal and to unveil your own spiritual mastery.

In humble and divine service,

Lavanya

My Early Years

As a young child, I was skinny and crossed-eyed. An uncle used to lovingly make fun of me and call me ugly. I outgrew being crossed-eye but I had a lazy eye that would wander when I was tired or stressed. Years later, I would hide my eyes behind sunglasses and even wore them indoors, hoping that no one would notice my imperfections. A beautiful soul once had the courage to ask me why was I hiding behind my sunglasses. I slowly began to heal from my sense of ugliness and began to embrace the beauty of the soul.

Also as a young child, I remember hearing from my mother and siblings that I would wake up every night screaming and talking to the thin air and that I would walk up to the mirror and tell myself that I was ugly. My mother took me to a psychologist when I was about 8 years old and I remember being impacted when the psychologist told my mother, "She is a perfectly normal child." I was impacted because I realized that my mother thought that there was something wrong with me.

On the day that I turned 12, I cut from school to hang out with a "friend" that I had made several weeks earlier. He was 13 years older than me but for some reason I felt important when I hung out with him. On my birthday, he raped me and my whole life dramatically changed. I decided to keep the incident a secret… but soon after, my parents would discover that I was hanging around with an older man. He would be summoned to my home and questioned. He informed my parents that I was no longer a virgin.

Because I had befriended him and willingly went to his house on that fateful day, the incident was not considered a "rape." My distraught parents did not know what to do. After seeking counsel, they were advised that in order to protect my integrity and have my violator assume responsibility that I should live with him.

I had a beautiful baby girl when I was 13. Although she would be one of the greatest gifts of my life in later years, she was anything but a gift in my early years. I had no idea how to take care of my precious angel and I had no idea what life was about.

At the age of 15, I realized that I had choices and I plotted to leave my daughter's father—my violator—whom I had been living with since the discovery of his actions. I left him and ran away with my daughter to my sister's house... and then the real nightmare began. My daughter's father became enraged. He stalked and tortured me emotionally and physically, hoping that I would return to him. One day he took my daughter, who was only 3 years old at the time, out for the day. He never brought her back. For the next year, he would send me photos of her, dirty and un-kept and the emotional pain was unbearable.

Soon after, the police became involved after discovering that my daughter's father had a lengthy and violent police record. As a trained marine, my daughter's father had plotted to abduct me and had converted our old apartment into a prisoner's trap where he planned to keep me after he caught me.

Afraid for my life, I moved from one relative's house to another. By the grace of God, several months later, my daughter's father committed another violent act and found himself compelled to run. He dropped my daughter off at a relative's house and after a year of not seeing her, I finally had my daughter back. It was a very challenging time in my life and getting her back in the condition that I did was horrifying, to say the least. It was obvious that she had been neglected, emotionally and physically.

I had taken a job at a moving company which paid me $75 to work 40 hours a week. I was also going to night school to earn my GED and the combination of all the stress, combined with having my daughter back was too much for me to handle. Thanks to a beloved cousin, who was like a sister, and who I was now living with, I had someone to take care of my daughter while I went to work and school. Still, the pressure of it all began to surface and one day, I began to suffer from shortness of breath and a serious bout of hives.

For almost a year I was in and out of hospitals. My hives became so serious that I could not breathe. My body was covered with huge, painful hives and I would often wake up and not be able to open my eyes because huge hives had developed over my eyelids. The doctors would give me medication and then release me but what I really needed was emotional help. The past and the present were slowing eating me up alive.

One day I was inspired to start keeping a journal. I had no clue where the idea came from, although I now know that it was my spirit that was inspiring me. The journal entries were very helpful in assisting me to release a lot of the emotional toxicity that I had inside of me. Eventually, I was inspired to begin to write a "book," a fictional story about my life! Looking back, my story probably would have made a terrific reality show today! I never published the book... I realize now that it was also another tool for my Self healing.

I also now realize that my desire to write a book about my life at that time was merely a cameo appearance that my soul was making to let me know that some time in the future, I would write... however, I needed to do a great deal of growing, emotionally and spiritually before then.

The attribute of Acceptance

As A Young Woman

At the age of 22, I was on my way to conquering the world, at least I thought I was. I earned my GED and began college at night. I began working as a bank teller and shortly after got promoted to the accounting department. This opportunity would greatly open the doors for a job in Wall Street several years later. This new leap would further contribute to my climbing out of the dark abyss but by no means did it mean that I was healed. I was still an emotional mess; I simply learned how to mask it and I chose to cover my pain by becoming successful and powerful in the physical and professional sense.

My daughter was doing better as years passed but my constant absence in her life surely had an emotional impact on her. I felt justified in many ways to feel resentful and angry at GOD and at the world. I was struggling to work and to study and I was responsible for taking care of my daughter when I was still a young woman myself. I had missed out of my teenage years of life and wanted to make up for time lost. When I got to Wall Street, I worked hard but played hard as well, all at my emotional expense and that of my daughter's.

I began to go out after work and to drink. I am so grateful that I never became an alcoholic or that I was never intrigued by drugs. However, in my own way, I was being destructive and I did not care. I did love my daughter dearly but in my mind I justified being out because I deserved it. I had suffered and lost out on enough and now it was my time to enjoy and reward myself for all of my hard work.

We are always given angels to help us through every step of our journey. For me, my angel at the time was my cousin, Irma, who was more like a sister to me. Irma and I moved in together after I got Brenda back and she would become a second mother to my daughter. In spite of the fact that I was not home a lot, I was comforted to know that Irma was taking care of my little girl in the best way that she could.

The Attribute of Perseverance

My Relationships

At 23, I became involved with a police officer who was 15 years older than me. We moved in together along with my daughter, Brenda. We managed to maintain the relationship for almost five years. This man was an instrumental part in my awakening because he reintroduced God to my life. I cannot remember for the life of me what the sect or belief was called but it had nothing to do with mainstream religion.

The philosophy of its teachings presented a spiritual GOD that existed within all of us and that was attainable through devotion and direct communion. I remember being intrigued by the concept and soon after, began to receive home lessons. Little did I know that George was the catalyst that would open the doors to my spirituality. God bless him.

Brenda did not get along with George and this began to cause serious problems in our relationship. Brenda, now 12, was doing poorly in school, cutting and hanging out with the wrong crowd. I was thriving in my Wall Street job and was required to work long hours into the night. I was struggling to keep a balance between work and home, never mind keeping track of Brenda. As the years had passed, Brenda's father had reappeared in our lives. He had reformed himself to Christianity; was now married and living in Puerto Rico and had expressed an interest in being in Brenda's life.

As it became a greater struggle to work and to keep Brenda under control, her father suggested that I send her out to live with him in Puerto Rico. I struggled deeply with the decision to send her away but at the end, I felt that perhaps the stability of a family with a religious foundation and the setting of a new environment would benefit her. When Brenda turned 13, I sent her to live with her father in Puerto Rico.

Shortly after, I was promoted to a managerial position in my

Wall Street job. I was proud of my achievements and worked and played very hard in order to prove myself to others. My relationship with George was dwindling to nothing. I had discovered a whole new world of excitement and fun and he became boring and unfulfilling. In spite of this, I was pushing him to marry me; after all, we were living together for almost five years. Smart man that he was, he kept reminding me of our age difference and refused to appease me.

I was doing lots of traveling on business and one fateful day I was to meet the next catalyst and helper in my life. While on business in Puerto Rico, I met Craig, who was vacationing there from Brooklyn. In my innocence, I saw Craig alone in the pool and asked him to join me and my staff. It was a perfect scenario since I was traveling with three women and one man. Little did I know that within hours of meeting Craig, I would become involved with him. For the first time in my life, I experienced a true connection and excitement about being in a relationship with someone who was my age and who was as ambitious as I was.

I continued to see Craig when I returned to New York and George knew that our days were numbered as soon as I returned from my trip from Puerto Rico. While I was there, I spent time with Brenda and was shocked to see how much she had transformed. She had been enrolled in a Christian school and her entire disposition had changed. She was no longer cursing or dressing provocatively but was now displaying a mild and humble side that I found almost uncanny. When I returned home, Brenda would often send me lengthy letters that talked about God and Jesus and she often shared her deep yearning for me to find God. She would always end her letters by telling me that she was praying for my soul.

After my breakup with George, I lost all sight of God again. Craig and I moved in together after dating for about six months and another whole world began to emerge. Craig was Jewish of faith and it did not appeal to me at all. It was a good excuse to abandon God. Both young and ambitious, we did a lot of traveling together, visited casinos and clubs often and we were living life with reckless abandonment.

The Attribute of Faith

A New Baby, A New Life

After living with Craig for about 6 years or so I awoke one morning feeling very sick. I swore I had a horrible stomach virus but as it turns out, I was pregnant. The news came as a surprise to me because I was using birth control but obviously my Jonathan wanted to enter this realm and chose me and Craig as his parents.

My relationship with Craig was stable in the sense of security; he was a good provider. However, we had begun to drift apart, mainly because of the misery Craig was experiencing for several years at his job. Time and time again, I had asked him to quit his job before it killed him but he would not listen.

In time, it began to kill our relationship. Another thorn was the fact that I had wanted to get married and Craig was hesitant to do so. We were engaged but there was no room to discuss marriage. Now pregnant, Craig finally agreed to get married but I always felt cheated by the whole experience and I resented the fact that he was probably only marrying me because I was expecting a child. We got married when I was four months pregnant and I was so unhappy that I could not wear a sexy dress because I was already showing.

Three days before my wedding I began to bleed and was horrified that I was having a miscarriage. The doctors assured me that the baby was fine but the experience was enough to put a cloud over my wedding night and honeymoon. Thankfully I stopped bleeding and several months later I gave birth to my beautiful son, Jonathan. He would prove to be a catalyst that would keep me away from work—and from the events of 9/11.

I was planning on returning to work after spending three months with my new baby. Yet, as the day approached for me to return to work, I felt heartbroken to leave Jonathan. I wanted to be the mother to him that I was not able to be to my precious

Brenda. The God Force must of heard my thoughts because on the day that I was scheduled to return to work, someone attempted to steal my purse while I was at the train station. I was punched in the face but luckily nothing was broken and I managed to hold on to my purse. I returned to my house and knew that there was a reason why that incident happened. For the next three years I dedicated myself to raising my son. I loved being a mother and I knew that I was trying to make up for all that I had not done for Brenda in my teenage years.

When Jonathan was four years old, I decided to go back to work on a consulting basis. My first interview back on Wall Street was on the day of the first terrorist attack on the World Trade Center. I was supposed to meet a friend for lunch at the popular Windows of the World restaurant. Luckily, I was detained in an interview and had to cancel my lunch date. I often look back to that day and know that I was being protected by the angels.

The Attribute of Devotion

My Spirituality Emerges

I was at home in between consulting jobs and I was bored and restless. My mother, who was living with me at the time, was watching a television program that was discussing the topic of angelic communication. At the time I had a very weak belief structure. I still had not reconciled with the God that had allowed me to have such a struggling and challenging life. Still, something about the program was calling my attention and I sat down to watch it. I thought the whole idea of communicating with angels was ridiculous, to say the least.

After watching the show, I decided to take a little cat nap and as I was laying in bed, the suggestions of the speakers on the show kept entering my mind. "Simply ask your angel a question." With an annoying feeling, I finally gave in to the meddling thought and I asked my angel for his or her name. In an instant the name Daniel seemed to appear in my consciousness. I thought it was odd but without another thought, I turned around and went to sleep.

The next day I went out to run some errands and when I returned home I had a message on my recorder. The message simply said, "Hey, it's me, Daniel. Call me." When I heard the message I did not piece it together immediately but about 30 minutes later I realized that the previous day when I attempted to ask my angel to identify himself, the name Daniel had popped into my consciousness.

The message that was left on my recorder did not include a phone number; it simply said, "call me." I felt a pulsing excitement move through me as I replayed the message over and over. I was guided to lay down and meditate. I gently whispered into the thin air and asked Daniel if that was his way of validating that he was real. To my utter surprise, Daniel appeared to me in a translucent form. From that day on, and for about a year, Daniel became my spiritual companion. He taught me many things about meditation and energy. In time, Daniel brought along many companions with him and for a year or so, I had the company of several angels with me that literally spoke and taught me many things about the spiritual realm. It all seemed unbelievable and yet, I knew it was real.

Daniel eventually shared with me that I needed to begin to write. I protested and complained that I had no writing skills. Daniel assured me that I needed to trust in his message and simply sit down and write. I followed his guidance and to my surprise, I was able to compose several articles on angelic communication. Daniel then guided me to go on the Internet and find a site where I could showcase my articles.

I was so afraid to share my articles because I did not have confidence in my writing abilities. Still, the process of finding a home for my articles manifested quickly, just as Daniel had said. I began to showcase my articles on a portal called Religionquest. In my articles I shared my own personal encounter with my angel and I began to receive many emails from readers who also had similar experiences.

I also received many emails from readers who felt that I should be mindful about communicating with beings that were not Jesus. Many of these letters stated that I could very well be communicating with the devil. I was thrown into a state of doubts and fear as I read these letters. My early fears from childhood and my fears of a punishing God came pouring out of my soul. In my desperation and confusion, I stopped writing my articles and I began to do in-depth research on biblical scriptures. To my horror, I found several references that confirmed what the readers were warning me of… that we could only speak to God or the angels through Jesus!

This was my first initiation into spirituality and the dark night of the soul. I was confused and anxious. I was lost. I was afraid to reach out to Daniel and all the angels that had lovingly nurtured and guided me for over a year. In my attempt to save my soul, I began to compose a book that spoke of my experiences and that also warned readers to be wary of any spiritual contact that was not made through Jesus. I found a publisher who accepted my manuscript but days before it went into print, I had a epiphany. I realized that it was impossible for Daniel and these loving angels to be evil. I realized that this was all a gift and a challenge to see if I would betray my own spirit and knowingness.

I attempted to stop the printing of my book but the publishers threatened to sue me. I knew that I had written the book for myself... that I needed to go through a dark night of the soul in order for my spirit to prevail. Shortly after the book was published, I put it out of print. I have never promoted the book... I wrote it for myself.

The Attribute of Trust

The Ultimate Test of Faith

My spirituality had emerged and I was on a roll. I read countless of books on the subject of meditation and devoted myself to the practice several times during the day. I was inspired to begin working on a new book and I was filled with inspiration and bliss. I had begun to share my spirituality with friends and family and the general consensus was utter surprise at my radical transformation.

I was graced to have begun sharing my spirituality and experiences with my beloved daughter, Brenda, who was now 22 years old and living in Las Vegas. We would spend hours talking on the phone about angels and spirituality. Although all of this spiritual talk was new to Brenda, she was happy to see that I had finally made peace with God.

This peace with God would be sorely tested and challenged upon Brenda's next phone call. She was calling to share with me that she had been experiencing a nagging cough for several weeks and she had decided to go to the doctor. At first they thought that she had a bad case of bronchitis but after a couple of doses of antibiotics and no relief, they ran some tests and diagnosed her with Lung Cancer.

Brenda was calling to ask if she could come to New York and stay with me in order to seek another opinion from Sloane Kettering. I told her to come as quickly as possible and reminded her to remain positive and focused. I had no idea that I was in the midst of one of the most challenging spiritual initiations that I would experience.

As soon as Brenda arrived, I introduced her to the manuscript I was composing for my book, "The Path that Leads the Way." I shared with her all the insight I had received from Daniel and from a God that I was still acquainting myself with. I shared with her the insight that emotions could cause disharmony in the body because that was spirit's way of telling us that there was evidence of spiritual blockages in the form of toxic emotions. I also shared with Brenda that we had the ability to create intentions that could literally change the course of our lives. Brenda was very open to listening and to learning. She eagerly began to read my manuscript as she began treatment at Sloane Kettering.

As time went by, I quietly struggled with my spirituality. I was in immense conflict because I knew that what I was writing about in my book was true. I also knew that there was a higher power that we could commune with and that would help us along the journey of life. Still, I was devastated and heartbroken that my little girl was going through this experience. I was gently told by Daniel that I needed to practice lovingly detachment. I was told that I needed to become a teacher for Brenda and not be a mother... For, if I acted as a mother, I would surely collapse into a deep state of despair.

Brenda became an eager student of spirituality and we would spend hours and hours talking about emotions, manifestations and creation. I introduced every exercise that I was inspired to create to Brenda as a tool that would assist her in healing her emotional wounds. In the meantime, I continued to work on my book and Brenda's progress was very promising. She had finished a course of chemotherapy and the doctors felt that her cancer was in remission. We were grateful and happy.

The Attribute of Courage

The Rite Of Passage Begins

One summer evening I began to feel sluggish and tired. Brenda was doing good and I was happily working on my book. Life seemed good. That evening, as I prepared to go to bed, I began to feel nauseous and dizzy. I decided to lay on the couch in case I got sick. As I laid with my eyes open, I suddenly began to feel this dreadful feeling come over me. I could not explain what the feeling was; it simply was dreadful and heavy. As the feeling of uneasiness intensified, I called upon Daniel to help me. I remember having my notebook next to me, as I often made notations after meditating. Daniel appeared to me and told me not to worry. He told me that I needed to have faith.

As I listened to Daniel speak, a strange noise caught my attention. The noise was coming from the bathroom and so I struggled to get up to investigate. As I walked to the kitchen to reach the bathroom I could see a flood of watering coming into the kitchen from the bathroom. When my feet touched the puddles of water on the floor, I had this overwhelming feeling that I was about to enter into a powerful and challenging experience. I was feeling weak but managed to clean up the mess. As I walked back to the couch I noticed that my equilibrium was off and that I was feeling very unbalanced. I crawled to the couch and grabbed my notebook and suddenly I was prompted to begin drawing strange symbols that I had never seen before. I was very aware that something was happening to me physically but that something was also happening to me spiritually.

I can't remember how long I was in this state that evening but what I do remember is that this was the first night that I had a direct contact with the God Force. This supreme and divine energy was speaking to me in a language that I did not have to understand. I remember barely being able to hold my notebook in my hands and still, I was prompted to draw symbols as I received a translation of energy that was being fed to me energetically.

The next morning I was severely ill. I had a crippling and ripping pain in the back of my head and I was unable to raise myself from the pillow. When I attempted to get up I had absolutely no balance. Craig rushed me to the hospital that morning and I was immediately quarantined. The doctors feared that I had meningitis. I remained in the hospital for several days and during that time they conducted every conceivable test to see if they could isolate my condition. The doctors insisted that I have a spinal tap in order to see if I had Lymes or Lupus. The spinal tap showed a high concentration of protein in the spinal fluid; an indication of a viral infection... and yet all my tests came back negative. I was sent home with a bag of medication and with no diagnosis. Although the nausea and dizziness eventually subsided, the pain in my head and my balance were still severe. I became very weak and would sleep for most of the day. I remained in a debilitated state for more than six months. I went to see specialists and went back to the hospital a handful of times, and still no one knew what was wrong with me.

At times, I felt as if I was truly dying. I could barely keep my eyes open for more than a few minutes and this was without taking any medications. I believe now that I needed to enter into this deep state of stillness and unconsciousness in order to receive the insight and gifts that would develop several years later. I also believe that during my sleep state, I traveled out of my body in order to receive mentoring and teachings from the Masters. Although I had little recollection of any of these teachings, I KNEW that I was being mentored.

Over the course of several months, I slowly began to recover from the feelings of exhaustion. I could get up from bed but my vision was blurry for many weeks. I had to have assistance in order to walk or I would support myself by pressing my hands against the walls. It is truly amazing to revisit this time in my life and to be sitting here, writing about them. I must admit that there were many times that I thought I would never recover from what I was experiencing.

My family and friends were still very concerned about me and the suggestion was made that I go see a top neurologist in New York. I made an appointment reluctantly, having the knowingness by now that this experience was truly a spiritual transformation. The specialist ordered a new set of MRIs and ran a battery of tests. A few days later I met with him to discuss his findings. The specialist had my MRI of my brain on the lit screen when I walked into his office and I took a breath. He reported that my MRI was normal and had no evidence of anything that would cause the symptoms that I had. He noted that there was an abnormality in my brain but that I was born with it and although abnormal; it was not correlated to my condition.

I asked the doctor what my abnormality was and he walked over to the lit screen and pointed the center of my forehead. He said that I had a hole in the middle of my head! When I realized where the hole in my brain was, I knew immediately that I was being given a sign that my condition was completely spiritual... the hole in my forehead is exactly where the third-eye chakra is located.

The attribute of Humbleness

Brenda's Transition

By the time autumn rolled in, I was feeling much better. I had gained enough control over my equilibrium that I could walk again and my blurry vision had diminished substantially I still suffered from the pain in the back of my head but I slowly began to learn how to live with the pain and still function. Throughout my ordeal and spiritual transformational, my family had been so supportive. Brenda, although still busy with appointments and attending to her own health, had been a wonderful inspiration. She would daily write note cards and letters to me, reminding me that I had a great mission to fulfill and that I needed to get better.

Brenda was doing well and seemed to be in remission. She began talking about going back to school and perhaps studying nursing. We were both very happy and grateful to have a reprieve from the challenging year that we had just faced together. Soon, the the holidays were upon us and Brenda began to experience anxiety at the thought of seeing the family for the holidays. When I asked her why she was anxious, she shared that she was concerned that people would want to talk about her cancer and ask her how she was. I reminded her that she had to believe that she was fine and that if people asked her, she should simply express her truth, regardless of what they thought.

Yet as the holidays neared, Brenda's concerns increased and suddenly she began to develop a hacking cough. By the time the holidays arrived Brenda was manifesting symptoms of bronchitis. And just as she suspected, everyone was concerned for her and everyone inquired about her health. By the end of the holidays, Brenda was compelled to return to the hospital and she was told that her cancer had become active again in her lungs.

Two weeks after New Years, Jonathan developed a severe case of the measles. He was running very high fevers and was miserable. Brenda was keeping regular appointments at the hospital and was trying with all her might to stay positive although her cough was getting progressively worse. One afternoon she decided that she was going to remove the ornaments from the Christmas tree and put it out. I asked her to wait for me to help her but that it needed to be later in the evening because I was spending time with Jonathan because he was so sick.

Brenda insisted on working on the tree on her own and as she began to move around the tree she realized just how labored her breathing was. She became depressed and for the first time in a long while, I felt torn between her and Jonathan. A few days later a visiting nurse came to see Brenda. I was out and when I returned home, I was horrified to see that the nurse had brought Brenda a portable ventilator. When I walked into her room and saw her sitting down with an oxygen mask over her face, I had a deep clutch of pain in my heart... I knew that this was the beginning of the end.

I desperately tried to remind Brenda that she had to release any fears that she had about her health. I pushed hard to remind her that she needed to do an inventory of any emotions that may still be blocking her wellness and wholeness. Brenda looked at me helplessly and assured me that she had released and reconciled with all of her past emotions.

The next day Brenda had a scheduled appointment at Sloan and I decided to go with her. I now realize that I was guided by the angels to accompany her. The doctors examined her and took some x-rays and when they returned to speak with her they had a grim look in their faces.

Brenda's primary doctor sat down next to her and told her that there was nothing else that they could do for her. The doctor said that she probably had one more week to live. I immediately sat down next to Brenda and took her hands in mine and told her to not listen to the doctor. I looked into her eyes and told her to look at me and to not put any energy into what he was saying. I thanked the doctor and kindly asked him to leave us alone. Brenda tried to put up a good front for me but we both knew that she was slowly preparing herself to depart. Brenda was sent home.

Two days later, she was feeling very labored in her breathing and she returned to the hospital. In the meantime, I was still tending to Jonathan and I could not spend the entire day with Brenda in the hospital. That afternoon, I was sitting with Jonathan, playing with Clay and I was inspired to create a butterfly. I am not usually very creative with my hands but the butterfly was so pretty that I decided to take it to Brenda that evening. When I gave her the butterfly, she lit up and said to me, "Oh it is me... I am transforming!" Little did I know that her soul was telling me that her transition had already begun.

Another two days later, Brenda was still in the hospital and I was at home, tending to Jonathan. I was planning on visiting her later in the evening and had spoken to her several times during the morning and afternoon. Around five PM, I was planning to start dinner but before I began, I took our little puppy, Buttons, and put her in her crate. Buttons, a little Lapsa, was only a few weeks old and she was tiny. She could walk but could still not climb up or down the stairs. It was recommended that we keep her in a crate at certain times during the day. I placed Buttons in the Crate, took her upstairs and placed a sheet over the crate.

I went back downstairs to start cooking and a few moments later I swore that I heard Buttons collar bells ringing not too far from me. I thought to myself that it was impossible... I had just taken Buttons upstairs. I heard the bells again and as I followed the sounds it led me to the living room. When I walked in I was shocked to see that Buttons was sitting in the middle of the living room floor. I instantly knew that Brenda was sending me a message... that I needed to get to the hospital immediately.

I made some frantic phone calls and within an hour I was at

Sloan Kettering. My beautiful angel was waiting for me to arrive. When I got there, Brenda was unconscious and I could tell that her spirit had begun to lift out of her body. I gently sat next to her and held her hand and placed my other hand on her heart. I silently spoke to her soul and told her that it was perfectly OK for her to let go and go home. I told her that I was proud of her and that I loved her very, very much and I asked the God Force to assist her in her journey home. A few minutes later, I felt this pulling energy in Brenda's chest. The ventilator made one final sound and then my baby's spirit lifted to heaven.

Brenda left me an amazing gift that would deeply comfort me after her passing. She had become an avid journal writer. After her passing, I found myself compelled to start going through her belongings, hoping to find some comfort in a piece of clothing that may still have her scent. Instead, what I found was several journals.

At first, I felt strange going through her private writings, but then I remembered how many times Brenda had shared with me that she was using the journals to post the many wonderful experiences and visions that she was having as she expanded in her spirituality. Brenda had become so attuned and opened to the spiritual realm that she would often complain about being awoken in the middle of the night to write down messages for me.

When Brenda first shared this with me I felt that it may have been dreams that she was having. However, as time went by and the messages continued to come, I realized that she was being used as a powerful catalyst to deliver messages to me. At the end of her physical life, Brenda's journals would prove to be one of the most incredible gifts that she could give me.

In her final entries during the last week of her physical life, Brenda shares how she was taken to a beautiful place, a place that was lush and green with bushes and trees. She also shares that there was a beautiful green pool of water the middle of the forest.

In her words, she said that she was guided to the pool on several occasions and that it felt absolutely divine and serene. She said that she was asked to enter the pool if she wished to. However, Brenda stated that she was not ready yet.

It was clear to me that the beautiful emerald green pool represented a portal to the afterlife. Brenda explains how there were several angelic beings of light waiting for her by the pool, all gently and lovingly guiding her to enter the pool if she was ready.

On the day that Brenda transcended, she had her journal with her in the hospital. The last entries captured her inability to write coherently; her final entries were scattered across the page. However, in the final moments, she shares that she sees the green pool of water and finally feels ready to enter it. She is greeted by two angels and she immerses herself in the water of rebirth.

This journal became a beacon of validation and of strength for me. I knew that my angel had completed her mission on this plane and was now home...being healed and taken care of by the angels. I kept the journal close to me and read it often. One day, I got careless and took it outside my backyard to read. I forgot to bring the journal back in with me and shortly after, it began to rain. Some of the journal entries became smeared but Brenda's account of her transition will forevermore live in my heart and soul. Thank you, my angel, for confirming what I already knew...

The Attribute of Observation

Time to Come Out Of The Closet

So much had happened in 2001. The events of 9/11, coupled with dealing with my illness and Brenda's final days were almost too much to bear. Brenda passed on January 23, 2002. I was left with a whirlpool of emotions about my spirituality and life itself. Still, I knew that there was a calling for me to fulfill and Brenda had made sure that I got that message before she passed… she would further remind me after she transcended.

A few weeks before Brenda's passing, she had shared with me her desire to return to school to study nursing. However she also was very interested in pursuing a holistic career. As a means to encourage her further, I immediately got on the Internet and started searching for distant learning programs that offered holistic venues. I found several interesting programs in Pranic Healing, Holistic Medicine and Spiritual Counseling. I printed out all the information and I created a colorful folder for Brenda. She was very excited at first when she saw all the material. Then a few days later, she came to me with one of the flyers that I had printed for her. She handed it to me and told me that she felt that I should enroll in the program. The program was for Spiritual Counseling.

I was surprised when Brenda told me that I should pursue the program. I felt content working on my book and in becoming a Reiki Master but, as she pressed me to begin this program, I began to feel some excitement. I also felt guilty that I was so excited because I truly gathered all the material to encourage Brenda to pursue one of the programs.

Now that Brenda had passed, I understood why she had insisted that I complete the certification for Spiritual Counseling. I also understood that it was my spirit that truly guided me to gather the material—for myself—even though I thought it was for my daughter. I did not get this message though, and so

Brenda became the messenger and the catalyst that would set me on track with my life's mission.

I completed my studies and earned my certification as a Spiritual Counselor. As I continued to witness all the pain that was surrounding the world with the events of 9/11, I knew that there was a need and a calling for spiritual healing. I began to ponder the idea of coming out into the world by setting up a private holistic practice. Still, I was very concerned about how people would react to holistic and spiritual modalities. My pondering became an obsession that I could not shake and I begged the angels and God for guidance. Then one day in the middle of August, I asked my beloved Brenda to give me an undeniable sign if she felt that opening up a practice was the right thing to do.

I meditated and asked her for help and then I went to run some errands. Upon my return, I went to check my mailbox and when I opened the box, a huge butterfly came flying out and landed on my nose. I instantly knew that it was a sign from Brenda... I recalled the day that I took her the clay butterfly and she announced that it was her! I had gotten the blessings from my angel to move forward with my calling.

I spoke to Craig about my idea and he had hesitations about its success but nonetheless offered me his support. I began to look for an office and must admit that I was very afraid to begin this new journey. I also began to feel discouraged when landlords would turn me away after I attempted to describe what a holistic practice was. By divine orchestration and with the help of my beloved daughter, it would be that my hair stylist at the time, Mary—who I found through Brenda because she felt I needed a new hair stylist—would be another catalyst in my life.

I went to get a haircut and was discussing my desire to find an office for my practice with Mary. She told me that the salon had an empty office in the basement. She spoke to the landlord, Joe, who was an amazing man, and he agreed to show me the office. As soon as I walked in, I knew that I had found my holy space... there was a huge mural on the wall of the Twin Towers. I broke down in tears when I saw the mural and Joe eagerly agreed to rent me the office space. He had absolutely no problems with the holistic work that I was going to do.... what a blessing.

The Attribute of Joy

Another Spiritual Initiation Begins

I was excited beyond measure to open my practice but I was also very afraid. I was afraid of how I would portray my work and myself to people. These feelings of doubt and fear would serve as a powerful but painful initiation for me. For almost a year, I sat alone in my sacred office and although some incredible miracles and revelations did take place towards the end of my first year in practice, I spent the first few months fighting and angry at God. I was angry at God because I found myself wondering if I had been led to open the practice just for myself; to prove that I could do it; just like when I had to write my first book for myself. I wondered where were all the people that I was shown that I was going to assist. Was it all an illusion?

During the first six months, I had to put into practice all of the exercises that I had written about in "The Path that Leads the Way." I meditated for a good part of the day while I sat alone, waiting for someone to come. Joe, my landlord, had a prestigious salon upstairs and he would periodically walk clients down to introduce me and my work to them. Most of them immediately wanted to know if I did "psychic readings" and I would take offense to their questions and immediately respond that I was a healer and a spiritual counselor. Little did I know that my offense to being asked if I did readings would come back to bite me in the butt in a very big way in later years.

My friend, Mary, who helped me to get my office, was a hair stylist upstairs and she would often come down to keep me company. She would also send clients down to meet me. One fateful day, she would send someone down to meet me who would forevermore change my life... and who would also help me expand my spiritual gifts in ways that I would never imagine. The woman, distraught beyond measure, had lost her son. She was suffering deeply and was desperate to find some peace after the loss of her son. She shared some details of her son; that he was a fireman and that he was a very beautiful young man. She never told me his name because she kept referring to him as "my son."

I shared with this devastated mother that my role as a healer was to act as a vehicle to the God Force to bring healing to a willing individual. I told her that as long as she was willing to receive, a healing could help in releasing a lot of her emotional pain, bring comfort to her and help her to re-energize. I also counseled her about the important process of allowing ourselves to grieve and I gently shared my personal spiritual philosophy about the afterlife and told her that our beloved past ones were in a peaceful state and very present in our lives, although we could not always feel them if we were experiencing a lot of emotional pain.

The woman listened and agreed to receive a healing treatment. I asked her to lay on my healing table and to relax. I played some relaxing music and, as usual, prepared myself to become open to the divine energies by taking a deep inhale and exhale. I asked the God Force to align me with its energy and to utilize me in any way that it deemed necessary in order to help this woman. When I felt ready, I approached the woman and placed my hand on her forehead. For a few moments, everything seemed normal. I was high in the energy of light, simply acting as a conduit for the energy, when suddenly I thought I saw something with my eyes closed. I opened my eyes for a moment and then closed them again. There again, in my mind's eyes, I could see an image of someone.

It was a young man, wearing a fireman's uniform. I could clearly see the company's number on the fireman's hat. I could also clearly see the color of his eyes and hair. He was standing in front of me, holding a small white dog. The fireman was smiling at me with a gentle face. Then without moving his lips, I could hear a voice in my mind that kept repeating, "Michael, Michael, Michael."

I must have opened and closed my eyes a dozen times, but every time that I closed them, I would see the same image, the same spirit, looking at me, almost as if he wanted me to do something. I began to panic because I did not know what to do with this information.

Memories of my past came racing through my mind. I remembered all the letters I got from readers warning me about obstructing energies when I wrote to share my experiences with my angel, Daniel. I wandered if something similar was happening. What was this, I asked myself. I feverishly began to pray and to ask for guidance and it was then that I received the insight to go grab a pen and paper and to jot down all the details of what I was seeing and hearing. I was asked to complete the healing but to focus on the details of all that I saw and heard so that I could later share it. Share it, I asked? With who? I was told that I should tell my client what I saw.

I was horrified and afraid beyond words. How can I explain to this grieving mother what I just saw when I could not even fully understand it myself? I was nervous and continued to pray for guidance. I completed the healing and as instructed, I took a pen and paper and wrote down all the details of what I saw and heard. I walked over to my client and asked her how she felt. She seemed to be much more relaxed and peaceful than when she walked in.

She was gracious and said that she felt lighter and more peaceful. It seemed like hours were passing by when only a few moments of silence came between the client and I. I was being pushed to share with the woman the details of what I had seen but I was so afraid. I can't really remember how I started to share the details with my client but I was authentic with her and told her that something that had never happened before in a healing had occurred.

I told her that I had seen the image of a man wearing fireman's uniform. I could immediately see that the woman became excited and wanted to hear more. I told her about the white little dog and she told me that the family did indeed have a white dog some years back but that it had passed away. For some reason, I chose to tell her next that the man kept repeating the name Michael. She immediately said that her father, who had passed, was named Michael. But then I began to describe the appearance of the man that I saw and her entire demeanor began to change from that of excitement, to that of confusion and doubt.

As I described the image that I saw, the client kept nodding her head in confusion. The description that I was sharing with her in no way matched that of her deceased son. She seemed a bit frustrated and disappointed because she had no idea who I was describing and I was even more frustrated and confused because I had no idea as well and I did not have more details to help her figure out who this was. I apologized to the client and told her that I thought it was her son. This statement only seemed to disturb her more. I felt mortified and was anxious for the woman to leave so that I could have a big cry and then a huge fight with God.

When the woman left, I sat down in complete dismay and emotional pain. Why on earth did I listen to that inner-guidance that told me to write all that I saw down? How could something so terrible happen? Now I knew for sure that people would not trust the process of the work that I was doing. Still, I could not deny that I saw what I saw and heard what I heard. What was it anyway? I had no idea what had just happened but I promised myself that I would never again allow this to happen again... and of course, the God Force heard me and had a good laugh!

I shared my experience with Mary and how sorry I was about what happened with the client that she brought down. Mary was very supportive and told me not to worry. Unfortunately, worry was all I could do. I had no explanation for what had occurred and now I had questions and concerns about my work. I meditated and asked for clarity, for answers, but nothing was revealed... that is, until three weeks later.

The Attribute of Grace

The Guru of Validations

Every one of my students will tell you that I am the queen of validations. I LOVE validations and teach my students to always give honor and reverence to validations. Validations are so important because they give divine creditability and authenticity to all that is unseen or unexplained in physical terms, but that can only be measured in spiritual truth!

My initiation and reverence to validations commenced when I was struggling to understand what had occurred that fateful day when I saw an image in my mind's eye and could not confirm with my client what I had seen or what it meant. Three weeks later, I was driving to the office and something told me to stop at a donut shop that I had never visited to get a cup of coffee.

I walked in to the shop and ordered a cup of coffee and as I waited, my eyes caught glimpse of a newspaper that was laying on the counter. In the right hand corner, there was a small photo with two people holding a picture in their hands. I could not see the picture clearly and something was nudging me to pick up the newspaper to take a closer look. Curiously, I picked up the newspaper and took a look at the picture. It was strange; the face in the picture looked familiar. I decided to quickly read the story and, as I did, I completely lost my breath.

I ran out of the coffee shop with a mixture of anxiety and excitement all at once. I did not know what to do. I sat in my car with my entire body shaking. The story in the newspaper was about a deceased fireman's parents who were grieving the loss of their son in the 9/11 events and who were now even more distraught because the city had announced the discontinuation of searching for remains. The parents were desperate to receive word of any remains from their son in order to have a proper burial ceremony. Their son's name was Michael.

I remember racing home and having a thousand thoughts

racing through my head. What do I do now, I asked myself? I could not piece together every part of this unfolding puzzle but one thing was clear to me... the image who I saw when I was giving that client a healing was definitely the same person in the picture in the newspaper... and his name was Michael! The spirit who spoke to me that day kept repeating the name, Michael, Michael, Michael.

I went online and did some research. My first stop was to the fire engine company where Michael worked. I found the email address of the chief and immediately wrote him an email. As I started to write the email, a fear started to surface. What about if they think I am crazy? How do I explain to the chief what I need to share? Will they come and lock me up? I tried desperately to find an address, phone number or email for the parents of Michael but I was not successful. I was anxiously waiting for the Chief to respond to me because I knew that I needed to speak to someone and tell them that Michael had contacted me spiritually and wanted his family to know that he was OK.

Several days went by and I had still not heard from the Chief. In my desperation, I contacted the client who had been the catalyst for this message—and also for the development of this sacred sense of insight for myself. I was afraid that the woman would not speak to me. By the grace of God, she was willing to take my phone call and to listen to the pieces of the puzzle that had unfolded since her visit to my office.

It was indeed an amazing validation to many spiritual truths. Once I mentioned the name Michael and the story in the newspaper, the distraught mother had an aha moment. In her desperation to receive a message from her own son, the client had not pieced together any of the information I had given her on the day she came to see me. Now the woman was able to help me to solve the mystery. It seemed that Michael and her son were very close friends. And although her son did not come through, Michael saw her as an opportunity—as a vessel—that could pass on the message that he was OK!

My life and my mission changed that fateful day. I realized so many beautiful things. The most important thing was that the afterlife surely exists; that our beloved passed ones are very much alive, peaceful and happy. I learned that I had to trust and step out of the way when it came to my divine work and that I should not limit the potential for anything divine to occur. I learned how to pray and to have faith. I also learned to have courage and boldness to speak with authenticity, all in the name of healing and of spirit.

What I did not learn that day was to fully accept the new insight that was emerging through my work. Although from that moment on, I would always keep a notebook handy whenever I was conducting a healing in case I received any messages, I was still uncomfortable—-(and am still working on it) trying to describe what this part of my work was. In time, I became comfortable with the word "Seer" but I would fringe every time somebody asked me if I was a medium or a psychic. I did not want to be labeled and above all, I only wanted to be a healer and a teacher.

The Attribute of Boldness

Yogananda Steps into my Life

During the onset of my spiritual awakening, my only teachers were my guardian angel, Daniel, the legions of angels that came to me for a year and my daughter, Brenda. I never had a guru in my life; someone who mentored me personally. My Reiki teachers attuned me distantly and, even though my attunements were very profound, I always felt a little cheated that I never had a physical guru in my life. I considered Neale Donald Walsh and John Randolph Price my gurus because I learned and grown immensely from reading their wonderful spiritual books.

So it came as a complete surprise to me when the Guru Yogananda was introduced to me and more specifically, the dramatic and transformational shifts that would follow. I was having a conversation with a colleague one day, exchanging spiritual philosophies when he mentioned the Yogananda's name and his incredible book, "The Autobiography of a Yogi."

I had no idea who this guru was and, although I was open to listen to my colleague share with me how amazing this guru had been, I came back with my personal opinion that Neale Donald Walsh was more of a contemporary teacher and guru. I will never forget the look in Prasad's eyes when he told me that I should read the autobiography… there was a twinkle in his eyes that was very intriguing and mysterious. I agreed to read the book in the future.

However, the next day I was giving a healing to one of my first students of the path, Mindy. When we completed the healing, I walked over to Mindy and the first words out of her mouth were, "have you ever read the Autobiography of a Yogi? I stood in disbelief at her question and immediately knew that it was not a coincidence that I was being invited by two beloveds in less than 24 hours to read this book. The next day I went to Barnes and Nobles to look for the book.

I was becoming frustrated in looking for the autobiography of Yogananda; I could not find a copy. I asked an assistant for help and she looked in the computer and confirmed that they had one copy. However, when we walked over to the section where the book supposedly was, she could not find it.

In frustration, I thanked her and started to walk away. A few moments later I heard the attendant's voice calling, "Miss, Miss, I found it." In that moment, my heart stopped and I knew that there was something about this book that was going to change my life forever. When I looked at the lovely face on the cover of the book, I felt a surging energy building in my heart. I felt a deep overwhelmedness of joy; a feeling that I could not quite explain. I took the book home but could not open it or read it for several days. I was afraid because I KNEW that this book was going to dramatically shift something within me. When I finally picked up the book, I could not put it down. I had the sensation that every single word was vibrating and moving through me as I read.

In the opening chapters of this incredible book, Yogananda shares a story about how his mother was told that her son was going to be an amazing healer and guru to the world. As she sat in meditation, receiving this insight about her son, miraculously, an amulet appeared in her hands. She was told that she was to give the amulet to Yogananda at the appropriate time and that it was intended for him to further develop his mission as a healer and guru.

I remember reading this story and immediately feeling an incredible exhilaration running through my veins. I felt an immediate resonation to the story and in a moment, I fell into a meditation pose and begged the God Force to gift me with an amulet. I asked the God Force to demonstrate to me that I was meant to be a healer and teacher and that if this was my mission, to prove it to me by giving me an amulet. I sat in my office, prostrated in a meditative position for what seemed like forever.

I cried and pleaded but the amulet never appeared. Hours

later, I got up feeling exhausted and defeated. I also felt betrayed and angry at the God Force for not providing me with the proof that I needed to keep moving forward. I was losing my faith in the practice since very few people were coming. I needed proof that this was my mission and God had failed to provide it for me.

The next day I came into the office depressed and unmotivated. Here I was again, to spend hours and hours by myself. I decided to work on packaging some glass chip stones that I had purchased to create little chakra kits. I sat there numb, putting the bags together when suddenly I dropped one of the little chips on the floor. When I bend down to pick it up, my eyes made contact with something a few inches away.

I wondered what it was as I got closer and suddenly I felt a deep sense of grace in my soul. Sitting on the rug was a beautiful emerald green glass stone but it was not a chip; it was about two inches wide and two inches long. It also had ripples going across the stone. I picked up the stone and in a moment knew that it was my amulet!

My green stone was the validation that I had asked the God Force for. I could not get to my feet. I crawled into my office and knelt in front of a Yogananda's photo that I had purchased and gave him my gratitude.

My Green Amulet

The Attribute of Pureness

Mythical or Mystical?

My passion for Yogananda became insatiable. I read every book that I could get my hands on to learn more about this beloved guru. I felt a deep love and connection to him that was unexplainable yet magical. I meditated every moment that I could and would ask the Guru for clarity and understanding. A few weeks later, my prayers would be answered but with the answering of my prayers also came a deep state of confusion and spiritual turmoil.

My student Mindy had often spoken to me about her first teacher and how spiritual and ascended she was. Mindy had shared that she had spoken to her about me and just in time to answer my prayers, Sandy (not her real name) was inspired to give me a surprise visit. It was a quiet afternoon when my doorbell rang at the office. I opened the door and Sandy introduced herself. We hugged as if we knew each other for forever. I invited her to come in and as soon as she saw Yogananda's photo on my alter, she knelt in front of him in reverence. I was elated to see that Sandy knew who the Yogananda was and I eagerly began to share my deep and mysterious connection to him.

Besides being a gifted spiritual teacher and healer, Sandy also was a talented numerologist. As I told her of my experiences, she listened with attentiveness. After a pause, Sandy asked me if I would share my birth date with her. I told her I was born on 2/6. When I told her, she stopped for a moment and then began to jot down some numbers on a notebook. The numbers read as such:

1/5, 2/6, 3/7

The dates respectfully represented Yogananda's birth date: 1/5

My birth date 2/6

And Yogananda's date of transition (death) 3/7

Sandy smiled warmly at me as she showed me the sequence of the numbers and told me that I was born in between Yogananda's birth and death; that I was his spiritual "daughter." I was so excited to see and understand what Sandy was writing on her notebook but when she told me that I was Yogananda's spiritual daughter, I became very confused and anxious. She then asked me for my full birth date: 2/6/1963. She shared with me that there was a sequence in numerology that determined a soul ascension path. She shared with me that the numbers that made up a birth date were added across and always deduced to a single digit to determine the Soul Path number. Finally, she shared that anyone with a soul path number of 9 was an ascended Master and Teacher. With all of this said, Sandy added the numbers of my full birth date: 2+6=8+1=9+9=18 (1 + 8=9) 9+6=15 (1+5=6) 6+3=9.

I admitted that I found the numerology presentation fascinating and that I was honored that my birth day numbers added to 9 but I was still very confused. Sandy then went on to jot down another series of numbers:

1/5/1893= 1+5=6+1=7+8=15 (1+5=6) 6+9=15(1+5=6) 6+3=9

This birth date belonged to Yogananda and it also added across to 9. Now I was more confused and even more anxious. I simply did not understand what all these numbers meant or what they had to do with me or the Guru. Sandy, seeing my anxiety, simply asked me to accept the great attunement that I had with the Yogananda. However, I wanted to share more with Sandy so I decided to tell her the magical story of my amulet. Again, she listened intently and when I finished my story I showed her my green stone.

Sandy's eyes were glimmering with knowledge and approval as she admired the stone. She shared with me that while on a trip to a sacred land (I truly cannot remember where), she met a wise sage who told her a story about a group of masters that would travel around the world to bring knowledge and healing. The sage had told Sandy that these masters would be known because of their humanitarian and healing work; they would possess a green stone. Sandy then noticed the ripples in my stone and noted that there were 9 ripples on my stone.

Needless to say, I was floored and speechless. However, I was also extremely overwhelmed because I still did not understand what all of this really meant... if anything at all. Soon after sharing all of the amazing knowledge that she had, Sandy said her goodbyes. I was—and still am—and will forevermore be grateful to this beautiful teacher and her messenger, for although I did not understand much of what she explained in that moment, everything that she shared with me would forever change my life and mission.

The aftermath of learning all that I did about Yogananda and the sequence of numbers in our birth dates, the stone, and the sage were almost too much for me to bear. My ego got in the way and I began to feel a deep sense of overwhelmedness and at the same time, a deep sense of denial; denial because I knew that no matter what all of this truly meant, it was pointing to a direction for me to ascend higher in my spirituality... and I was simply not ready to take0 that leap. I was not ready because I still had blockages of unworthiness.

I need to pause at this point because the many experiences that followed that fateful meeting with Sandy are enough to write a whole volume, all on its own. I will add, however, that in its climax, I was so in denial to align myself with the gifts that Yogananda was offering me that on several occasions I thought it would be much easier to contemplate suicide than to have to accept what was being revealed to me.

In retrospect, this was all part of my initiation into mastery. In time, I did align myself unconditionally with the Yogananda's energy and I humbly accepted the gift of assimilating and holding whatever teachings I needed to hold in order to be a beloved guru for others. Today I humbly but boldly display a photo that reflects the images of the Yogananda and myself as One.

The Attribute of Gratitude

Memories of Past Lives

Once I aligned myself to the energies of the Yogananda, a whole new spiritual realm began to emerge for me. My practice finally began to blossom and I was blessed beyond measure to be gifted with an assistant, my pillar and a great ascended master herself, my Sea. Sea and I met in the most unusual circumstances and in a very short time I had the blessing of having her join me at the Spiritual Path. To most, she was my assistant but to me she was my pillar, a great teacher and protector.

In Sea, I found a confidant that I could share all the amazing revelations that I was experiencing. To my grace, Sea was very ascended and actually able to help me through many challenging times in my own spiritual ascension. My spirituality, insight and awareness began to increase very rapidly. I began to channel and to receive insight on many realms of existence. I began to have memories of my past lives; many of which were intimately connected to other civilizations and timelines.

I was also able to identify and see the matrixes of other people's past lives and many other things. My healings became very powerful and I actually had to stop offering hands-on healings for a while because the energy was so intense that people could not withstand the heat from my hands. It was all very beautiful, challenging and mystical.

With Sea's help, I learned how to ground myself while I was learning how to harness all of these new frequencies. I was doing fine until memories of being in Egypt in a past life came to surface. I realized that with all that I had grown spiritually, I still had some judgments about certain religious beliefs and cults. I felt that the Golden age of Egypt had a strong connection to magic and I had a resistance to remember and accept that I was certainly a part of those times. Sea helped me tremendously to reconcile with my old patterns of perception in order to align myself to receiving whatever I needed to from that golden age.

In truth, it was never only about me; it was more about allowing myself to assimilate the memories and energies of past lives so that I could hold those energies and then help the many who would come to me with memories of other time spans. Many of us come into this realm with a number of attributes that we mastered in past lives but we simply do not remember those lives. It was in this role, as an Activator, that I would later assist many to complete their spiritual puzzles by being able to help them to identify their past lives. In doing so, these individuals would be able to re-activate many attributes and gifts from their past and also begin to harness the alignment for their mission in life.

It was my memory of being a shaman in a past live that allowed me to reconnect to the knowledge, wisdom and connection that I had with Mother Earth. In this lifetime, I had very little training in shamanism but humbly I say, it was not necessary, for in my past memories I found all the training and knowledge that I needed to become a powerful shaman in this lifetime.

The assimilations of my past training as a shaman enabled me to expand the spectrum of my healing energies to assist others. I was guided to offer soul retrievals to individuals who desperately needed to reunite with fragmented aspects of their souls that were energetically left behind in traumatic events in past lives. Because Shaman healings are greatly in alignment with the potent energy of Mother Earth, the healings are very grounding and can greatly facilitate the healing of the structural body. I was—and continue to be—a humble witness to the healing of many structural conditions in the body of many clients and students.

One of the greatest healings I was able to be a witness to was of a beloved student of mine at the time. She had come to see me in hopes of receiving some relief to the constant and daily pain she was experiencing; she had been battling with Multiple Sclerosis for several years. The beloved was in so much pain that she wore braces to support her neck and knees.

In our first session, I gently but firmly shared with her the importance of recognizing the connection with illness in the body and emotional blockages. I told her that healings would certainly help her to refuel and revitalize but that healings alone would not necessarily heal her. I said this—and still share this powerful truth with my beloved ones because ultimate healing can only come when we rid ourselves from the toxic emotions and separation that we create for ourselves when we are holding on to toxic emotions.

Of course, I will also add that I WILL never limit the Divine and that the potential for miraculous and spontaneous healing can certainly occur. However, if we do not shift and change our patterns of thinking and our emotional behaviors, in time, an old or new illness can develop. This is so because it is the TOXCITY and blockage of emotions that primarily causes disharmony in the body.

Getting back to the beloved with MS, she was very willing to begin our work together. And sure enough, as we conducted some of the powerful exercises that help in reconciling with emotional blockages, we discovered that as a child, the beloved had been ridiculed for her weight and also criticized for desiring to pursue an artistic desire to paint. Having isolated these deep-rooted emotional blockages, I was able to guide the beloved one to reconcile with these painful emotions and to reclaim herself. The combination of this emotional work, along with powerful Shaman healings, assisted the beloved to heal completely from her MS.

She not only was able to wean herself off her medications and no longer need the supports of braces for her body—she defied modern medicine and was able to undergo MRIs that no longer detected the lesions that were found in previous MRIs years later. Her dramatic recovery was such a miracle that her doctor of many years humbly shared with her that her spontaneous recovery had led him to reconsider retirement from his profession.

Although this segment was supposed to be dedicated to discussing my experiences with past lives, I feel it was important to share with you this incredible and inspiring story of healing. It is important and relevant to past lives because I am sure that I would not have been able to assist this beautiful person to heal in the way that she did had I not remembered all that I had learned and all that I had been in my past lives.

There is no 'attribute of' line here – should there be?

Other Civilizations and Light Beings

I had begun to get more comfortable with my ability to channel but I would limit it to becoming a vessel for it only to receive insight. I would sit down and allow myself to lift from the body and enter a higher state of consciousness and then I would have Sea sit with me and take notes as I channeled. It was during this phase of my ascension that I recognized beyond a shadow of a doubt that there existed other civilizations—more evolved—than ours. During the commencement of my channeling, I made contact with a highly evolved Atlantian who helped me tremendously in working with the Atlantian energies that many possess in this realm.

As I allowed myself to become open to be of service in this arena, beings from other highly evolved civilizations such as the Pleiadians and Arcturians began to come in for sessions. It was truly amazing because it was as if they were directed to find me once I allowed myself to harness the energies that would help me work with them.

I met many beautiful beings of light that actually walk among us as "normal humans" when in reality, they are highly evolved beings that are here to hold and carry the energies of love and light for humanity. For the most part, these beings came to me because they needed to have their seals of memory activated. Many of them are carriers of great knowledge and insight. I had the immense privilege of working closely with an Arcturian who became an amazing mentor and teacher for me.

Ray (not his real name) initially sought me out because he was being plagued by other energies and needed help. Ray was one of the most loving and beings that I had—and have ever met in my life. He was incredibly soft-spoken and in the beginning of our work together I felt extremely challenged because I felt like I needed to literally pull information out of him in order to help him.

For several sessions, Ray would sit in front of me during sessions and simply look at me. I would attempt to begin a dialogue but he would enter into a trance and then would begin to morph right in front of my eyes. In the beginning, when these events began, I would excuse myself from the office and run out to Sea and tell her that I did not know if I could work with Ray. Sea would always ground and remind me of my mission and I would eventually make it back to my office.

Ray was being tortured by energies that he claimed would latch on to him energetically and keep him from attaining freedom and mastery of his own mission in life. In describing his experiences, it seemed like Ray was stuck in between realities or realms and that these energies wanted to stop him from being activated because if he succeeded in becoming free, Ray would become a powerful vessel for humanity. Over the next two years I worked very closely with Ray. Through healings, spiritual exercises and a lot of trust and faith,

I was guided to conduct a soul retrieval on Ray with the assistance of several of my students in order to help release him from the energies that were constraining him. It was truly a miracle to witness Ray's transformation. The soul retrieval was successful and Ray eventually reclaimed his spirit and became a powerhouse. He began to share his insight about the cosmos, the shifts that were taking place and also began to mentor and prepare me for the next initiation. Although I was happy to see Ray in possession of all his divinity I was not too happy to learn that he was going to become a tough teacher for me!

At the time of Ray's arrival and transformation, I believed that I was living my mission and fulfilling my purpose in the highest degree possible. Thanks to the financial support of Craig, I was able to move from my little office and establish the Spiritual Path. Within the sacred new space I had created a beautiful storefront that carried all things spiritual. In addition, I had attuned and taught enough students to be able to also have a room where students offered meditation classes and that I would use to offer workshops. I was so happy with all that we were accomplishing as a team. Still, at the end of the day, I was becoming depleted because I was seeing an average of four to five clients a day, five days a week. I was trying to encourage my students to join me in offering healings and counseling to people but it never truly came to fruition.

Once Ray was in alignment with his Arcturian energies and knowledge, he began to discipline and prepare me for the future. He shared with me that I was going to go through one of the toughest initiations yet and that I needed to prepare myself emotionally, physically and spiritually. He also told me that I needed support in my work because that many were going to come to seek help. I felt frustrated by his words. I was tired and I felt that I could do no more than I was. I was also angry that I was being told that I was going to go through yet another initiation; a rite of passage. I asked the God Force why was it that I needed to endure and suffer so much if all I was trying to do was to be of divine service.

Some of my students were touched by Ray's announcement that I needed more support in the Spiritual Path and also for the work and mission that was coming. Without too much sugar-coating he told my students who were working with me that if I did not receive the support that I needed, other beings would come to my assistance to help me bring the Spiritual Path to where it needed to be.

This declaration was a spiritual Ouchy for the staff students who had been with me for several years but that obviously had gotten comfortable and stuck in their limited roles as meditation teachers. They, too, were being called to mastery. But the most challenging experience was yet to come. When it walked in through the door, it not only shook the very foundation of the Spiritual Path... it brought completion of many contracts with some of my most beloved students, it also brought an end to my marriage and almost broke me spiritually.

The Attribute of Authenticity

The Twin Flame Field

I had no idea what Twin Flames were and I had no interest in knowing. However, the God Force had other plans and I was going to have to learn very quickly what Twin Flames were or else I stood the risk of compromising everything that I had worked so hard to achieve. Ray had warned me that my greatest initiation was going to come but, after losing my daughter, I felt that I could endure anything and withstand the pain, and also prevail. Yet, the combination of emotional challenges that I was yet to experience truly came close to breaking me spiritually.

One fateful day, a man name Steve walked into the Spiritual Path. He was interested in learning how to meditate in order to help with his focus. I happened to be available and standing outside the boutique when Steve came. We talked for a few moments and I shared a few of my philosophies on the connection between emotions and physical disharmony. I told him about healings and he was very interested. I had an opening a few hours later and this is how our journey began.

Steve experienced a miraculous healing from a painful neck injury on his very first visit to the healing table. He had not shared with me that he had suffered an accident when he was a fireman that had left him with severe neck injuries. He had learned how to live with the pain. Once I got him on the healing table, I was intuitively guided to heal his neck pain. Steve was sold on the spot and began to come on a regular basis for healings and counseling sessions.

Steve was also from the AA rooms and this had provided a pretty solid spiritual foundation for him. He was familiar with meditation and with the healing process. Through our work together, I learned that Steve was divorced and "available." I immediately began to try to set him up with a several of my students because I felt that he was a good catch. I had absolutely no personal interest in him. Although I knew my relationship with Craig had fulfilled its course, I was content to be happy with my practice and to keep my family together for the sake of my son, Jonathan. Craig was a very good man and a wonderful provider but as I had grown spiritually, it became obvious that our contract was coming to fulfillment.

The setup with my students did not work out. In the meantime I continued to work with Steve and one day I had an unexpected and impactful experience with him. I was teaching Steve about our Oneness with the God Force and I asked him to point out to me where God was. Steve hesitated for a moment and then answered that God was everywhere. When I asked him if he was God, he was impacted by my words and could not respond. I got up to get a mirror so that he could see the reflection of God within himself and when he looked at the mirror and then looked up at me, I was instantly thrown into a memory of a past life that we had shared together.

The experience took me out of the office and placed me in a wooded forest that was facing a creek with rocks. It was in a Native American ground. I was 14 or 15 years old and my family had been killed and I had managed to escape. I was hungry and dirty and sitting on a rock when a shaman appeared from nowhere and was standing in front of me. All in one moment, as I saw the scene in my mind's eye, I knew that this beautiful shaman had saved my life and stolen my heart. I was suddenly brought back to the office and Steve was looking at me with innocent and confusing eyes. I remember walking to him and hugging him but he had no clue why I was. I thought for a moment that perhaps Steve had seen and experienced the same vision that I had. To my dismay, he had not. I did not tell Steve what I saw.

I shared my experience with Sea and told her that I had a deep sense that Steve and I had not completed something in that lifetime and that we were being presented with the opportunity to complete in this lifetime. I was anxious and wanted to know more... and as we must be careful for what we ask, I began to have a flood of memories about our past... and it was extremely painful. All the while, Steve had no clue about any of this. I had not shared any of the visions that I had and he just continued to come in for sessions and to work on himself.

I was very puzzled by what I was tapping into; that I was being invited to commence a relationship with this man. For, although he was open and willing and he was also spiritual, but Steve had a lot of baggage, both emotionally and physically. He had three beautiful sons from two different relationships and he was still very entwined—emotionally and physically in the lives of his previous partners.

Steve needed a lot of polishing and I was not interested in investing so much time. I felt that if I had to harness another relationship, I at least deserved someone who was more up to par in his spiritual evolution than Steve was. And so, I hesitated and I resisted the call from the Divine.

Steve had taken an interest in the healing arts soon after his retirement and became a massage therapist. One day he invited me to come in for a massage. At first, it seemed like a good idea but on the eve of our appointment a great anxiety came over me. I was so anxious that I made up a white lie and canceled my appointment with him. My beloved Sea comforted and guided me so much through this crisis. She gently reminded me that if I was being called to honor a contract that sooner or later I was going to have to fulfill it. Reluctantly, I rescheduled my massage appointment with Steve, however, as soon as I walked in the door, I asked Steve if I could have a word with him. I can laugh at the thought of this now... I sternly told Steve that I wanted to make sure that we maintained strict boundaries between our professional work. Steve looked at me with a puzzled face, I am sure, not having a clue to what I was talking about! Of course, he agreed and I then prepared to receive my massage.

I went into an instant state of trance as soon as Steve began to work on me. I was thrown into that life time that we shared together and saw every detail of our lives. I learned that the Shaman—who was Steve—had indeed taken me back to his village where his people lovingly took me in and nurtured me back to health. I remembered that the Shaman was a powerful warrior and healer for his community and that he had chosen to teach me all that he knew. He was very tough with me because he wanted me to learn how to take care of myself.

I remembered that we fell madly in love and that we consummated our relationship in the most sacred way. There was tragedy as well. I remembered that there came a time when our village was being attacked. I was pregnant and my shaman came to me and told me to not leave the tent because he was going into warrior mode with the rest of the men. He gently kissed me on the forehead and then left. I would never see him again. The shaman was riding his horse and was attacked. In an attempt to escape, he rode up and fell off a cliff and met his death.

While I was viewing our past as I laid in trance, Steve was wondering why I was thrashing and mumbling so much. He later shared with me that I was by far his strangest client! I, of course, did not share any of what I saw but when I went to say goodbye to Steve I could not help myself and kissed him in the lips. Steve was a gentleman and did not attempt to take advantage of an obvious moment of vulnerability for me. He confessed to me later that as I walked away he found himself wondering why would I—such a refined spiritual guru—be prompted to kiss him.

Now I was conflicted. I knew that I was still married and that Craig did not deserve for me to violate our relationship. I was in turmoil because I could not tear myself from the painful memories of the past, much less block the insight that was telling me that I was going to have to trust and be courageous enough to share my truth with this man. I decided to write a lengthy letter to Steve, explaining all the details of what I had seen in hopes that he would have some recollection. To my utter dismay, Steve had no idea or memories about any of what I shared with him and instead of helping him, my truth threw him into an abyss of confusion and questions.

The gripping connection that I felt toward Steve was becoming unbearable and my beloved Sea would once again help me to understand the Divine connection between Twin Flames. In many ways, Sea was always a trigger for me. Once she would open a door of divine dialogue with me, the insight and recall of these subjects would be activated within me and I would suddenly have an understanding and knowledge of the subject.

This was the case when Sea and I discussed the Divine Field of Twin Flames. It is a lengthy subject that is deserving of an entire book dedicated to explaining the sacredness of such a union. It must suffice in this book to share that Twin Flames are two aspects of the same Soul molecule; two aspects of the same soul. The purpose in "separating" twin flames aspects was intended for the expansion of growth and ultimately, for twin flames to come back together through the participation of many lives to teach and reflect upon each other their mutual growth and lessons that still needed to be learned.

The ultimate goal of twin flames is to successfully unify, having satisfied the accumulative karma created in past lives and to finally be able to hold a unified field of Oneness for all of humanity through their own union of their souls. In summary, twin flames are a holy relationship because they represent the return and union of Oneness.

For this reason, a twin flame couple that can successfully reach spiritual union on all levels of existence is considered one of the highest unions that can be attained. This realization was what compelled me to continue nurturing the relationship and to endure all that was to come. It was by far, as Ray had predicted, one of my most challenging initiations; one that I desperately battled to fulfill in the name of unity for humanity.

The Attribute of Compassion

The Painful Rites of Passage

The initiation to become a holder of the twin flame field began to rip away at my life and as a consequence I began to experience a deep sense of vulnerability. Steve, although open to listening to the little spoonfuls that I was feeding him, was still experiencing a lot of physical and emotional blockages in his life. He was not ready to hold this sacred field of twin flames that we were being invited to step into.

I discovered that Steve was also still involved with his last partner, although not in an emotional way, he was still physically involved with her. I was still living at home, although estranged from Craig. It was truly a bloody mess. I was willing to walk away from all I needed to in order to nourish the relationship with Steve but I was not so willing to live with all of the physicality that he still had in his life.

The irony of it all was that Steve's raw energy of physicality was supposed to balance my extreme cosmic energy, and my cosmic energy was supposed to balance his primal energy. Of course, in the heat of it all, we were experiencing pain and resistance towards the balancing of our energies... we were doing this by operating on extreme opposite sides; I was ready to lift to the cosmos and he was comfortable moving and living in his physicality. Honestly, in many ways, we repelled each other although we shared an indescribable passion for each other as well. It was an incredible mixture of many emotions.

My vulnerability began to show in my work; I was crying and in emotional pain all the time. I had reached a place where I could no longer nurture the relationship and continue to experience the anguish of Steve's inability to devote himself solely to our relationship. He simply was not ready and I wanted out of this contract. I begged and pleaded for the God Force to release me of this burden. I begged for mercy and reminded the

God Force of how much I had already done for humanity and how much more I needed to do but might not be able to do if I continued in this toxic and hurtful relationship.

In my contemplation for answers, I was given a divine insight and alternative that would ease my pain but that would eventually be the cause of many more painful experiences. I was asked by the God Force to allow a beloved student whom I was grooming, to assist me by allowing him to step in and hold my field until Steve was ready. This revelation did not sit well with my staff students because they had witnessed how much I had suffered in trying to nurture my relationship with Steve. They protested and felt it was impossible for me to nurture a relationship with someone else. It was conflicting for them because I had always reminded them that I needed to stay with Steve no matter what because the relationship represented so much more than just our union.

Three of my closest students, who were an vital part of the Spiritual Path, unable to trust my insight and clouded by their judgments, all agreed to abandon their work at the center and to walk away from their guru at the same time. The three, children of my spiritual womb, all wrote me letters of disapproval and farewell. My heart broke beyond words.

My world seemed to collapse as I saw pieces of it crumbling right in front of my eyes. Not only did three of my disciples walk away to never speak to me again, but Craig had finally discovered that I was nurturing a relationship with Steve and was obviously very distraught and upset with me. Through all of this I kept begging God to release me from all the pain and to simply take me home. I was ready to go home.

My pleas were unheard. My life only got more complicated and painful. By the grace of God I had Sea to comfort me. Ray was also impacted by my decision to allow another to hold my field until Steve was ready and also walked away. Now I no longer had his guidance and support. Steve was terribly confused and angry when I told him that I needed to harness another relationship because I was being compromised by his unwillingness to devote himself solely to our relationship. I continued to work with him and in truth, our relationship never really ended but it was extremely painful and transformational to say the least.

Fast forward, through many painful experiences, Steve and I managed to overcome and prevail. We moved in together, got engaged and eventually got married—twice! My greatest joy is that in spite of all the turmoil, the loss of my students, the judgments and the ridicule, I was strengthened by my faith and devotion to fulfill a divine mission and I did. Against all odds, Steve and I overcame the many obstacles that we faced and succeeded in becoming One as twin flames in union and in divine purpose.

The Attribute of Tolerance

Ray's Predictions

Ray was absolutely correct when he predicted that a new collective group was going to show up to support the Spiritual Path. In the midst of my initiation to the Twin Flame field and as Steve and I embarked on finally working as a spiritual unit, a new group of students stepped in to the Spiritual Path.

The new breed of students began with the arrival of one beautiful young lady, who not so coincidentally, was part of a group of beings, friends and family, that all shared a desire to develop spiritually. Soon, one told the other about the Spiritual Path and in a short time, we had not only formed a strong collective group; but would recognize that we had all been a part of a larger collective family in previous life times.

By the way, I must add that at the time when the three students teachers left the Spiritual Path, many of my beloved students remained devoted and supportive to me and the center. These beloved masters in their own right still continue to be with me and some have risen to amazing heights in their own spiritual missions. You all know who you are... and I simply love and adore you for your eternal support and love.

Working with these students was very rewarding because most of them had a deep awareness of their spirituality and they also knew that there was a great calling to be of service. It was with this group that the God Force chose for me to truly emerge into Shamanism, teaching and working with the students to honor Mother Earth, to tap into the reservoir of the Oneness that existed between All and the Mother Divine. This was an incredible time because we knew that many earth changes and shifts were in the horizon.

At the heights of our spiritual contract, the group grew to a solid 20-25 students, all beautiful and luminous in their own light. They were all unique in their own way; some were Indigo, shamans and others were healers. There was a common denominator in most of them... there was a deep connection to the mystical place of Avalon and the priestesses of that time.

I was feeling happy and purposeful again and blissful that these new students were so powerful in their intention to be beacons of light. I had slowly come to the realization that a large part of my mission was to help those whom I was inspired to call the "Ascended Ones," old and experienced souls that had signed up to come to this realm in order to be great vehicles of light for humanity. In many ways, I felt like their spiritual mother and I was so proud of my children. Finally, I was able to begin to heal the deep wounds of losing three of my most beloved students... the universe had provided me with the a new flock of chelas.

I have so much to be grateful for to this group of Ascended Ones. They came at a time when I truly needed them in order to uphold the mission of the Spiritual Path. Their love and devotion allowed me to harness the Mother Divine Energy in such a natural way because I loved each one of them with my womb. It would come to pass that my contract with "my children" would also come to pass. This story, too, can be an entire book, all on its own. It must suffice to say that the group had received all the maternal love and support that they need from an Omega vessel. Through a series of events and also, the arrival of a beautiful Alpha Guru, who I invited for the students to meet, the completion of our contract came to a surprising and abrupt finale.

The re-opening of old wounds resurfaced again. My dream and deep desire to have a group of enlightened beings as part of the Spiritual Path had once again collapsed. My heart and womb were injured beyond words. I had still not learned that I had to let go of attachments and expectations. I also had not embraced the message that the God Force was trying to convey to me... that "I was" the Spiritual Path.

The Attribute of Vision

Earth Work through the Vessel

I have always advocated to my students the importance of recognizing that we possess the ability to be divine vessels for the God Force and for the healing of the Earth. I add that we may never completely know the extent to which the God Force will use us to deliver healing; it can be through our voice, through our creative expression, through our actions or through the literal use of our bodies that may serve as a vessel of light and healing.

During the monumental earthquake and tsunami in Japan, the earth experienced a literal movement of its axis. The consequence of this shift created a global shift in the earth's core and activity. This event quickly drew my attention because two years prior, I had received insight to travel to South America do conduct Shaman work on the land. Soon after I received this divine insight, the God Force sent me two powerful validations to confirm the insight. A beloved angel from Columbia came traveling from his homeland to Staten Island, NY, to find me. I had never had any prior contact with this young man and when he showed up in my office and shared that he was from Columbia, I knew that the God Force was speaking to me. The young man's name was Jesus.

Jesus shared with me that he was guided to find me and had come to receive Reiki attunements and teachings. The young man was a pure beacon of light and it was an honor to assist him to return back home as a healer and teacher. Jesus had shared with me the need for spiritual nourishment in South America and I told him that I was being called to travel there. A few weeks later, another beloved one sought me out on the WWW. Her name is Karol and she, too, was from South America. Karol lives in Chile and shared with me that she was guided to find me after having visions and dreams of me. She eagerly and anxiously wanted me to travel to her homeland.

Attempting to honor the divine calling, I spoke to my students and we organized a fundraiser event to raise money for the trip. Although the event was wonderful, it did not produce the funds needed to make the trip to South America. I was disappointed and a bit confused; for, if the God Force needed me to go to South America, why had we not raised enough funds to achieve the task? I reminded myself that everything happens in divine order and entered into a state of trust.

A year later, Japan experienced one of the most powerful earthquakes in history and along with it, a shift in the core of the earth. When this event occurred, I intuitively knew that I had to remain mindful of the moving energies. Soon after the earthquake, I was having a conversation with my beloved Mother, who lives in Puerto Rico. Mom shared with me that there was an unusual amount of tremors and earthquake activity on the Island, like never before. As soon as I became aware of these events, I knew that the energies that I was supposed to work with in South America had shifted due to the earthquake in Japan. I knew that I had to travel to Puerto Rico to do Shaman work on the earth.

The timing was perfect. For years, my mother and sister would celebrate their birthdays together. My sister's birthday is August 21 and my mother's is the following day. My sister, Gloria, who also lives in New York, would always travel to Puerto Rico to celebrate her birthday with Mom. I was always reluctant travel to Puerto Rico during this time of the year because the weather is extremely hot. However, I knew that I had to travel to the Island—not only to see my beloved Mother and to join in the celebration; I knew I had to go to serve as a vessel for the earth and for its healing.

Steve and I made our travel arrangements in May and Jonathan was also coming out with us. We were excited about the trip and we allowed ourselves to start making plans to go out dancing and touring around the Island. Little did we know that the God Force had other plans for us.

A week before our trip, I began to bleed and figured that it was my regular menstrual. However, as the days progressed, my bleeding became heavier and I began to get concerned. Two day before the trip the bleeding stopped. I was relieved and thankful. However, the night before our flight, I began to bleed profusely. It was truly alarming and I immediately entered into a state of meditation to receive guidance. I asked the Omega if I needed to seek medical attention or postpone my trip. I was told that I should not fear and trust that I would be OK to fly.

Our flight was scheduled for ten o'clock in the morning. I got up early and was horrified to see how much blood I was passing. Again, I entered into a state of meditation and again I was told to trust. It was only by the grace of my faith that I got on the plane. I must confess that I was afraid that I would bleed to death during my flight. Gracefully, the bleeding seemed to subside during my flight.

We arrived promptly and safely in San Juan, Puerto Rico and, after picking up our bags, headed to the rental car. As we waited for the agent to bring us our rental, we stood outside and noticed that there was an eerie silence in the air. We found it unusual that there were no people around. When the attendant brought us the rental car, I inquired about the quietness of travelers or people around. The attendant looked at me with a baffled look in her eyes. She then shared that everyone was preparing for the arrival of Hurricane Irene. The attendant was right in looking at us in the strange way that she did; we had absolutely no idea that we have just flown in to an Island that was preparing to be hit by a hurricane.

The news that a hurricane was headed to Puerto Rico was yet another validation as to why we were guided to come to the Island, and also, why I was bleeding so profusely. I have always been a "womb" vessel; a vessel that holds a great field of maternal energy in the womb to nourish and nurture humanity.

As a shaman, I also operate from the womb; offering my vessel to the Mother Earth to filter the release and receipt of energies. I knew without a doubt that Mother Earth was utilizing this hurricane to move and release energies from the ground and it was utilizing my sacred temple to assist in the movements of these frequencies.

We were joyfully greeted by my family at the resort that we were staying in for the week. It was so wonderful to see my mother, brother and the rest of the family. As we caught up, my family indeed confirmed that they were preparing for the arrival of hurricane Irene, which was scheduled to hit land in approximately 36 hours. The hurricane was predicted to enter Puerto Rico as a category 1. We spent a quiet evening with family on our first night before the winds and rain began to pour in.

It was raining intensely on our first full day in Puerto Rico and my flow was mimicking the fall of the rain. As much as I tried to remain in a place of trust, my concern over my physical wellness was beginning to increase. We headed out to my mother's early afternoon and about an hour after we arrived, I received guidance that I needed medical intervention. I approached my family and Steve and told them that I needed to go to the hospital. I could sense the concern in everyone. It was surprising to hear me, the guru who constantly supported that everything that manifests in the body can be healed spiritually and emotionally, had a need to go to the hospital. Nonetheless, my family and Steve were extremely supportive and in less than 30 minutes, I was taken to the emergency room.

The hurricane was upon us as we drove to the hospital. The winds were blowing about 50 to 60 mph. and we knew that the weather was only going to get progressively worse. After taking my vital signs and seeing that I was not critical, I was asked to wait. Almost two hours went by before I was called in to see the doctor. After taking down the details of my condition, the doctor ordered a sonogram and blood work. I was given hormones through IV to help stop the flow of bleeding. The doctor said that I would be at the hospital for at least six hours. My sister, brother and sister-in-law had accompanied Steve and me to the hospital and we asked them to leave before the brunt of the storm came. My family was so supportive; they went home and returned 30 minutes later with blankets and food to hold us up for the next few hours and then they drove through 80 mph. winds back home.

The rage of hurricane Irene began to pass through the Island as I laid in a hospital bed waiting for my results. Steve lovingly sat by my side, attempting to get a little rest from the hectic events of the day. As I laid in bed, I asked the God Force what was the purpose of this experience. I knew that I had to come to Puerto Rico and I had sensed that I had to do some shamanic work with the land... but laying in the bed of a hospital did not seem like shaman work, I thought. It was then that it was revealed to me that I was indeed helping Mother Earth with the cleansing and purifying that was taking place. I was reminded of the "womb" vessel that I was and was reassured that all would be well.

My tests results came back and there were no signs of cysts, tumors or any other condition that would cause the bleeding. My blood tests also came back good. The doctor could only suggest that perhaps my body was undergoing a hormonal change. I took an exhale of gratitude and felt that bliss and joy of being able to serve as a vessel for Mother Earth.

My family had asked the doctor to not let us leave the hospital until the hurricane had passed. We had been in the hospital now for over six hours. The doctor literally walked outside and took an inventory of the weather conditions before he released me. The resort that we were staying in was about 15 minutes from the hospital. Steve went to get the car and we began our journey back to the resort. About two minutes after we began our drive, the winds and rain began to rise with a fierce energy. It seemed that we were in the eye of the storm and as we began to drive, the tail end of the hurricane was upon us. I must confess that I experienced a moment of fear.

Steve had absolutely no visibility as he drove through hurricane Irene. The winds were blowing in excess of 80 mph. and there were trees down in every direction. As we drove, trees rocked with fierce force and it seemed like we were going to get crushed by falling trees. At times, the water was so deep in parts of the road that Steve had to maneuver the car in drastic directions in order to prevent the car from falling into a ditch of deep water.

All along the ride, I kept praying and fighting with the God Force. I was praying for our safety but also fighting with the God Force because I did not understand how it was possible for this to be happening to us when I was being a vehicle and vessel for the healing of the Earth. How could we be compromised in such a way, I protested! I had allowed myself to get caught up in a moment of mistrust and fear. I had not recognized that Steve, a shaman in a past life and a retired firefighter, was more than seasoned and prepared to move through the elements with focus and safety. I also had forgotten that the God Force had assured me that we would be safe. We made it safely back to the resort.

The next few days would be very challenging... and yet, very graceful as well. The hurricane had passed through the Island and had left its mark, but thankfully, everyone was safe. My mother and brother, who lived about twenty minutes from the resort, had lost their electricity and water supply. The resort lost electricity but still had running water. For the next two days, my family joined us at the resort and we made the best of it.

We made beds on the floor and others slept on couches but we were able to spend quality time together in spite of the darkness and silence of no television. My mother had no electricity but had a gas tank stove so we were able to go to her house to eat meals. In truth, this experience was very transformational for all of us because it taught us to appreciate the many things that we take for granted. It also allowed us to bond and to become humble together.

Still, there was another challenge brewing. While I was at the hospital, I had received an insight that I should return to New York with Steve. Our return flights were a day apart; Steve was scheduled to return a day sooner than me because his son was scheduled to report to his college in Upstate New York.

I shared the insight I received with Steve and told him that he needed to change my flight. I explained that I was told that he should not leave me and that I needed to return with him to New York. I was told that if we did not leave together, I would not be able to return on my scheduled flight back.

Steve spent some time trying to track the hurricane now that it was predicted to reach New York over the next few days. He tried to assure me that my flight was going to make it back to New York before the hurricane would reach the city but that was simply not good enough for me. The anxiety of needing to return with him had nothing to do with the hurricane; it had to do with the feeling of separation that I felt that was going to take place if he left first.

We argued about the flights. Steve called the airlines and there was only one flight available that would accommodate our return together. The flight had a layover in Georgia and it was scheduled to depart on Friday, two days before the hurricane was due to reach New York. However, there were some weather reports that were placing the hurricane near Atlanta to arrive Friday evening. Steve contended that it was unnecessary to cancel my trip for New York on Saturday because the hurricane was not scheduled to hit New York until Sunday afternoon. Steve left on Friday morning and, on Friday evening, the airlines canceled my return trip to New York. Because of the bad weather conditions across the states, my flight was rescheduled five days later.

I experienced a mixture of emotions during the next five days. Although I was not alone and I had my beautiful son, Jonathan, with me, and my family made sure to come visit me and pick me up every day during my extended stay, my heart was broken because Steve did not believe me when I told him of the insight that I received. I felt abandoned by him and I also felt vulnerable.

Although my bleeding had subsided, as a result of the emotional surge of the entire week and the obvious earth movements, I was feeling very vulnerable and heightened. Steve was supposed to be my grounder and protector and now he was gone and I had another six days in Puerto Rico.

This experience was very profound and liberating for me. Although I was sad that Steve did not listen to me and also felt abandoned by him, I had no choice but to pull on my own spiritual strength and I learned to not let the feelings of vulnerability weaken me spiritually. Jonathan was such a source of strength and encouragement for me during our extended stay in Puerto Rico and I realized that I did not need Steve to take care of me... I could take care of myself and the God Force would always provide someone to watch over me.

During the last two days of my stay on the Island, I was able to do extensive shaman healing work with Mother Earth. I was only a few blocks away from the ocean and would go to the waters and attune myself to the needs of the Mother Divine.

How ironic that I was not in New York when the hurricane arrived. I guess I was spared because I had already experienced the energy of Irene in Puerto Rico and I needed to replenish from the earthly and spiritual work that I did there.

I felt a new sense of connection to the Mother Earth that I had quite never felt before. Although the pieces of this experience may sound random to others, there is no doubt in my soul that the events took place exactly how they had to in order to allow me to partake in the healing of our beloved earth. I am grateful for the experience and would do it all over again if I had to.

It is interesting to also note that once I returned to New York, I visited a GYN doctor to follow-up. The doctor found no evidence of any imbalances in my hormones to explain the excessive flow that I experienced. I gently smiled at the news. I knew that in some beautiful and mysterious way, I was helping Mother Earth give birth to a new aspect of Her.

We can all participate in the healing of our earth. It is not necessary to undergo challenging situations as had occurred on my trip to Puerto Rico. Those events had a lot more to offer than just being a vessel. The events allowed me to re-connect with my family and with my son on a whole new level. They also allowed me to realize that I did not need Steve in order to remain strong and erected in my Shaman work.

The next time there is a prediction of a natural event approaching, go out into the earth and offer it your healing, love and light. Do not ever underestimate the amount of support and assistance that you can render by offering your loving energy and love to the Mother that supports our very existence!

The Attribute of Honor

The Master Must Have No Expectations

One of the greatest principles I teach and pass on to my beloved ones is to not have any expectations for the outcome of any situation or circumstance. There is a vast difference between holding a "field of *Intention*" and having an expectation. An intention holds the trust for an outcome but also takes into account the attribute of "Acceptance," the recognition that no matter what the outcome, we must honor divine order. Expectations are set upon specific outcomes that leave no room to honor the potential for another outcome. As such, expectations can set us up for immense disappointments.

It is especially difficult to practice acceptance and letting go of expectations when it pertains to the spiritual healing of those that we love and care for. In our heart, we would like to see each one of them reach a state of healing and of happiness. However, much as we may hold a field of intention, we also need to honor the choices that others make through freewill. I thought that I had mastered this attribute to a great degree, that is, until I experienced a very emotional and traumatic event with one of my beloved students.

Derek (not his real name) had come to me seeking spiritual guidance and development. At his present stage of life, Derek had reached a complete state of emotional paralysis. He shared that he had experienced a very challenging adolescent life that drove him to experiment with drugs. The drugs had helped to mask his feelings of misplacement in the world and helped him to escape his deep yearning for isolation. Derek's only escape was his love for music. He enjoyed playing the guitar and composing music. That dream ended when Derek was involved in a car accident that left him with deep injuries in his hands. Now, years later, Derek was on a host of medications for bipolar, manic disorder and depression.

Gracefully, Derek possessed a great hunger for spirituality and for healing. In a very short time, we worked on helping him heal from all the trauma of his past. Incredibly, as Derek healed, the walls of isolation and of fear began to dismantle. Within a year, Derek was playing his guitar again and, after several years of complete isolation, he had managed to break down the walls of fear and was also now working as a music teacher. It was amazing to witness Derek's transformation. I was very proud of his achievements and considered him to be a brilliant example of what spiritual healing could do to transform lives.

However, as time continued to pass, Derek began to manifest steaks of arrogance and instability. I reminded Derek of the importance of practicing humbleness and gratitude for all the transformation that he had experienced and achieved. For, no matter how successful we become, we must always remember to be pure and humble in all that we are.

Derek came to see me one last time. He came to announce that he no longer needed a guru and that he had hired a professional coach to help him develop an image for his music career. During the visit, Derek criticized my inability to promote myself properly and uttered many other comments that were painful to hear. They were painful to hear because in his words, I could see that he had completely disconnected himself from the Source that had helped him to heal.

I gave Derek my blessings and reminded him of the three principles that would always keep him in alignment with the God Force: Grace, Humbleness and Gratitude. As I gave him blessings, I saw a glimmer of humbleness in his eyes. I knew that moment that I would not ever see Derek again.

Several days later, I received a disturbing email from Derek. It was obvious from his graphic profanity that he was not emotionally stable. I chose to not respond to the email and instead, sent him blessings. A few days later, I began to receive phone calls from an un-identified phone number; the messages that were left were extremely disturbing.

My heart was filled with emotional pain. I could not believe that my Derek, who had transformed and healed in such an amazing way, was suddenly a completely lost soul again. I found myself experiencing doubts and guilt about my sacred work. I put myself under the spiritual microscope and began to question my discernment. It was surely a very challenging time.

As if this was not enough, a few days later, I received a telephone call from a local detective. He was calling to see if I had heard from Derek because his mother had made a missing person report. I was shocked to hear the news and shared with the detective that I had received several disturbing phone calls from Derek. He asked if I had saved any of the messages and I said yes.

The detective asked me to come to see him. He heard the messages and was disturbed to hear the vulgar threats and words that Derek expressed. Because of his medical past and diagnoses, the detective felt that the phone messages could be used to charge Derek with aggravated assault and that this would enable police to pursue him and place him under medical care for treatment. With maternal pain in my heart and womb, I filed a complaint and prayed that the police could find Derek before he hurt himself or someone else.

The next few days felt like I was having a nightmare that I could not wake up from. The police had tracked Derek in another state but had not arrested him. They knew that he had access to a car and that he was moving about. Steve and I had become heightened by all the news and events and did not feel comfortable staying at home. We packed a bag and went to stay at a hotel. That night, I asked all the angels to help bring clarity to Derek and to shield him with healing light.

The next morning, I received a telephone call from the detective. Derek had called his mother and was on his way back to Staten Island. He told his mom that he was going to admit himself to a hospital. The angels had helped him to see the light!

Derek remained under care for about two weeks. During this time, the detective called again to inform me that, due to his illness, the DA had not accepted the charges for aggravated assault . However, Derek had other pending charges and the detective shared that most likely, they would bargain with Derek if he agreed to enter a rehab program. I never heard from the detective or Derek again.

It took me a long time to reconcile from this experience. There were many times that I found myself asking if it was worth it to continue doing the work that I was doing if it was going to place me in such vulnerable situations. In a million years, I never thought that I would have to experience fear towards a beloved that I loved and helped to heal. I questioned my judgment. I doubted my work and, more than anything, I could not overcome the expectations that I had envisioned Derek fulfilling. How could I be so wrong, I asked myself?

In time, I realized that Derek's choices and actions did not have anything to do with my work or my teachings. His decisions and choices had been made by him from a place of spiritual separation and disconnection. My vision of what I saw in him was real; I saw Derek's potential and I held a field of intention and a reflection for him of all that he could become. Derek embraced the reflection but, in the process, chose to disconnect himself from the Source that had assisted him to regain his spiritual and emotional balance.

I learned from this experience that I can only hold a field of intention for others, but I must never allow myself to have expectations or ever forget that we are only a step away from falling out of grace when we separate ourselves from the attributes of mastery and the principles of healing.

The greatest gift that I received from this experience was to practice the attribute of forgiveness. I forgave Derek for all the things that he said and all the things that he did and did not do, and I also transformed my emotional pain into the energy of compassion. Finally, I forgave myself for putting myself under the radar, for questioning my purpose and mission in life and for allowing myself to measure the choices of one individual to blur the healing and transformation of the countless of beloved ones that continue to blind me with their radiance! Forgiveness is truly liberating and freeing.

The Attribute of Forgiveness

The Gypsy Spiritual Path

In the 11 years that the Spiritual Path has been in existence, the office has occupied five different locations and another move is in the horizon. When I moved the office from its first home to a larger space, it was a joyful move because it represented expansion. The Spiritual Path had a center for classes and also a holistic boutique. When I had to leave the center, I was devastated beyond words because I absolutely loved that space and cherished all that we had accomplished there.

My third move was due financial necessity. We moved to a beautiful space that resembled a temple and I did manage to do an immense amount of cosmic work there. Our location, though, was not very visible and in a short amount of time I was struggling to maintain the financial expenses for the space.

As a God Send, a beautiful colleague of mine—who had spoken to me a year prior about the potential of sharing her space—came walking in to my temple space in divine timing. I had not seen my beautiful Pamela in over a year and, as I found myself in turmoil, wondering what I was going to do, Pamela came to visit me. As a validation, she shared that a great energetic force almost forced her to come see me! It was the perfect solution and partnership. Pamela was a cosmetologist and nurse and had an extra office in her space. She graciously gave me her waiting room space to create a little pharmacy for my herbs and oils.

Pamela and I shared office space for a wonderful year and then my beautiful Pam became ill and passed away. The landlord wanted to me to stay but I was concerned with the responsibility of paying the rent on my own. I was becoming frustrated with the gypsy moves of the Spiritual Path and I found myself asking the God Force why did it have to be so difficult to maintain a sacred space for my practice when all that I was offering was in the name of healing and wholeness? I began to feel unsupported by the Universe.

Once again, a space would be provided by the God Force. A student of mine told me of a Spa/Hair Salon which offered holistic services. She felt that we would complement each other very well. When I visited the spa I knew that I had to establish my practice there even though I also knew that it would be temporary. I was surprised and a little apprehensive when several of my students shared their concerns about my potential move to the spa. I contemplated deeply and again received insight that I should move my office to the spa although it was going to be for a short time.

The move was a radical one in that my clients and students had always been accustomed to my providing "womb-like," intimate and sacred spaces for them. Although my office space at the spa was beautiful and sacred, there were other venues under the same roof and the flow of many clients throughout the day made it impossible to hold a serene and intimate environment for my practice. In time, many of my clients and students stopped coming for sessions.

The move was also a very radical change for my Sea, who had always had her own private space in each of the previous spaces. We remained at the spa as long as we needed to and when the God Force gave the green light to move, the next move would be even more drastic than any of the previous ones.

My next move—which is where I currently have my office— was to finally stop resisting and surrender to moving the office to my place of residence. For years the suggestion had been made but I always felt that I needed to have boundaries set between my office and my home. Still, at the time that I got the green light from the God Force to move from the spa, Steve and I were also looking to move from the house that we were renting. With so many moves behind the Spiritual Path, it finally felt right to consider moving my office to my residence. There were downsides to this new endeavor, however. The first and most painful one would be that I would no longer have Sea with me. After nine years of working together and holding the field for the Spiritual Path, moving the office to my home would not provide a space for Sea to work in.

As this shift took place, I realized that the predictions that I had been making for months—that radical changes were imminent—were now on our doorstep. Not only would I not have my pillar with me to take care of me, to nurture and buffer me, but I would also have to learn how to schedule my own appointments, be on time with my sessions (something that I had never mastered!), and also handle the fees, something that I was also very uncomfortable doing. I would also have to allow myself to become comfortable with letting clients and students to enter into the intimacy of my home space. Needless to say, this has been a most radical and transformational transition.

We make plans and the God Force laughs. We finally found the perfect home that would accommodate the office and still allow privacy of our home space. When I began working from home it felt uncomfortable at first but in a short amount of time I adapted. I loved the idea of being able to expand my hours now that I did not have to travel to and from an outside office. I had to learn how to become disciplined with my time management and also to improvise by using other tools such as texting and emails to schedule appointments. Although I miss my Sea terribly, I learned that "where there is a will, there is a way." Oh, and I almost forgot to share what I mean when I say that we make plans and the God Force laughs. So we found the perfect house and we decided to rent it for a year, with the potential of purchasing it at a later time. Just three months after we moved in the landlord announced that he needed to sell the house as soon as possible! Not being in a position to purchase it, we are enjoying the house as long as we could until it is sold... the Spiritual Path will surely be moving again!

The Attribute of Growth

What I Have learned

I have learned so many beautiful lessons and have grown so much in my spiritual journey! Every experience that I have shared with you has given me the opportunity to embrace one or more of the attributes that are presented in this book. I have also learned that every experience that I have partaken in has been a beautiful gift of grace; for I would have never arrived to the place I find myself in today were it not for each molecule of every moment that I had to experience along the way.

In addition to the many lessons and opportunities that I have received from my experiences, I also discovered that my initiations were all geared to help me understand and to see that I possessed many characteristics that were not in harmony with the attributes that create the foundation for mastery. Through my greatest challenges, I learned that:

- I had many expectations, which led to many disappointments
- I had many attachments, which led me to experience emotional pain
- I prolonged my spiritual growth by resisting change
- I believed I trusted when I lacked in faith
- I always questioned The God Force instead of looking at myself
- I believed I needed others to validate my Self-Realization
- I was unwilling to become expansive so I limited my growth
- I believed that my spaces were the "Spiritual Path"
- I believed I needed to be strong in order to prove my mastery
- I had to let go of everything and have nothing to find myself

- I am still a student of life
- My experiences created the foundation for my mastery

As I write these words, I am so full of gratefulness for all that I have experienced in my life. I am also humbled that I was given the opportunity to review the many pieces of my own spiritual puzzle in writing this book. Looking back at all that has transpired in my life has given me the opportunity to exhale once again and to "wipe and clear" any lingering residue as I revisited these parts of my past.

I have been reminded that the goal towards healing and mastery should not be approached with the expectations that life will suddenly be free of emotional challenges and become a bed of roses. This is not to say that we should simply succumb to experiencing emotional pain in order to gain mastery and to heal. What it does mean is that we recognize that the arrival of emotions in any form is always adorned with a golden opportunity to heal and to grow. Every emotional challenge is inviting us to embrace one or more of the divine attributes presented in this book.

There are clearly choices to be made along the journey to life and mastery. For the most part, we will have the ability to select which roads we will follow and, other times, our path will be directly by the choices of others. Yet still, hidden within the choices that others may make that directly impact our stance, we are invited to remember that in the spiritual realm, we KNEW that these choices could be made on our behalf... and still we agreed to partake in the journey, because we knew that every path would ultimately lead us to an opportunity for healing and growth.

When we can embrace this divine truth, we can then become the observers of our circumstances and life and truly reveal which gifts of growth are being presented to us. We can then arm ourselves with spiritual passion and devotion to harness whatever attributes are beckoning to be embraced by our spirit!

Mastery does not define perfection; mastery encompasses the ability and the will to excel in every moment of life. To excel is to grow and to expand even when the growth is composed of tiny baby steps and, even when we find ourselves stumbling and falling, if we get up and begin to move forward again, that is growth.

I have humbly learned from my journey that there are no mistakes in life. If we allow ourselves to become the observers, we can begin to see the weave that unifies an experience with a very important part of our spiritual puzzle. In time, if we also allow ourselves to heal from the toxic weigh of emotional debris, we can begin to see and understand the patterns that were connected; why things happened the way they did and why the "players" in our chess board game played out their strategy in certain ways. It is all part of a bigger chess game; the game of life.

This is not to say that life should not be taken seriously or that I am simply downgrading the sacredness of life to a mere game. Quite the contrary; life is a precious experience and our strategy to play our part in the game is very important because it will greatly determine how the game unfolds. However, through our emotions and our physical state, we often get stuck in a "move" within the game and feel we are unable to move forward. The greatest strategy is one that can be done from the eyes of the observer.

I am so thankful to the many souls who have played a role in my chess game of life. I recognize that each of them played a vital role in my growth and that their choices and decisions were all leading me to look at something within myself. Through their actions, I learned to find strength and trust. I also learned how to honor my emotions but to move beyond the grips of attachments to a place of spiritual freedom.

The great news is that we can all benefit from these divine truths. We are all capable of healing and growing from our experiences. The only protocol that is required is for you to be willing to let go of the gripping emotions that would like to declare you a victim of circumstances, and to arm yourself instead with the attributes of mastery. These attributes will surely assist you to mend and heal all of your wounds and will help you to build a wholesome foundation for your life and your spirit. The attributes of mastery will also help you to unveil your purpose and mission in life.

I pray and hope that the chapters of my life have served to inspire and uplift you. I hope that my life has touched your heart but also brought inspiration and empowerment to your life!

Today...

I have shared so many of my experiences from the past that have helped me to learn and grow that I feel that my story would not be complete unless I share with you where I am today in my spiritual journey.

Currently, I still have my beloved practice, The Spiritual Path, although I have come to recognize and embrace that "I am" the "Spiritual Path." The space where I conduct my sacred work no longer defines the value of what is offered, but instead, it is the energy and love that I bring to every session that creates the space... no matter where it is. My office is currently located in my home.

I love working from home because it allows me to spend time with my beautiful son, Jonathan. I am able to pick him up from school and connect with him over a cup of coffee in between sessions. I have been blessed with my son; he is a wonderful student in school and, although very shy and reserved on the external, he is a very sweet and energetically attuned young man.

I also love inviting my clients and students into my space and allowing them to experience the energy of love and spirit that is such a central part of my home life. In many ways, it is like having a beloved family member come over for an intimate visit. Sometimes the coziness gets me in trouble in staying focused on the time for the next intimate visit of another beloved.

Recently, I received a powerful message while having a session with a new person. I was sitting in front of her, listening to her speak and suddenly my whole body began to shake. For the first time since having my practice, I wanted to run out of the office. I had to do everything in my power to sit composed and to place my attention on the beloved catalyst that was sitting in front of me.

After our session, I was shaken and immediately went in to

contemplation. I demanded to know why I was feeling so unsettled. As we must be prepared to hear the answer to what we inquire about, I was told that I could no longer work with "little ones" on a one-to one basis. I was reminded that many times I was told that it was time to expand myself and to go out into the world to reach the masses. I was told that I needed to close my practice and dedicate my full concentration on workshops, seminars and promoting my books.

I was devastated when I received the answer to my question. For I love what I do; working with individuals and witnessing their lives transform. The God Force negotiated with me. It told me that I could still see my students on a one-to-one basis but that I needed to change the course of my mission. The time for this change is now.

I feel blessed to have found a partner who is opened to spirituality. Steve and I have managed to overcome many challenges together and have also created a field of balance of both ground and cosmic energy. Steve is a grounder and moves very well in the earthly realm. I, on the other hand, am very cosmic and experience everything from a spiritual perspective. Sometimes, Steve and I don't see eye to eye on the causes and effects of life. Still, I think back to all the emotional pain that we endured in order to be together and I am grateful that we managed to overcome the many obstacles. There are still many challenges that we face daily. Steve lives a busy life, having three sons from two different relationships. He also dedicates time to being of service as a counselor. This leaves very little time to nourish a relationship. However, I am thankful for what we have accomplished as a twin flame couple.

I am always so filled with anticipation and excitement at the release of a new book. I become excited because as I review the chapters and the vibration of the messages delivered by the Divine, I feel the infusion of unconditional love and guidance that the God Force is striving to deliver to the readers—and to myself.

I must admit that I also experience a little bit of anxiety when I am ready to release a book because I have yet to master the art of marketing and promotions. There is a big part of me that believes that anyone who needs to read my book will find their way to it so I have difficulties devoting time to promoting my books or myself for that matter.

For some time now, I have had a deep yearning and calling to spread my wings beyond the spectrum of seeing clients and students on a one to one basis. My soul has been pushing me to go out into the masses so that I can reach and help others more expansively. There is a huge part of me that feels ready to answer the call but there is also a part of me that truly loves the intimacy of working one-on-one with my beloved ones.

I recognize that this dilemma has kept me from truly bringing any of my books to the next level. I have become comfortable self-publishing after attempting to introduce my books to traditional publishers and feeling the disappointment of rejection notices. Still, I recognize—even as I was writing this book—that I truly need to stop making excuses and start getting my energy and messages out into the world!

And so, I AM READY. I am declaring myself! I am ready to come out into the masses! There... I did it.

I have also learned from channeling this book and from contributing a chapter of my own spiritual journey, that in the past, I have spent a great deal of time worrying about how I should define myself in my work and mission. I have invested a great deal of time obtaining certifications and degrees because I always felt that I needed to validate the knowledge and insight that I possessed with educational preparation that would be "acceptable" and deemed creditable in the eyes of society.

Although I am grateful to have obtained an educational basis for Natural and Holistic Medicine, I now realize that my greatest insight and knowledge has come to me from my soul and my deep yearning to be of service to the Divine God Force. Over the years I have battled to define what I "do" and what I "am" in order to feel accepted and validated.

I was afraid of being called strange or "weird" as my son playfully calls me. I would spend enormous amount of time trying to explain what I "see" when I look above someone's head and why I was jotting down notes to capture the "messages" I was receiving. People ask me what is it that I see or hear and I say, "nothing." I literally do not see or hear but I sense, feel and communicate with energy. It is an unheard and unseen energy but potently accurate in what it needs to convey. I have always been stern about not wanting to be called a "psychic" and would much prefer to be called a *Seer*.

I have also learned to honor and love the realm of the *After Life* and have had the immense joy of being able to act as a catalyst and channel for many beloved past ones who wish to deliver a message of hope and love. I cannot act as a channel for the Afterlife at *will*; it only happens when a beloved past one wishes to come through to deliver a message. For this reason, I also have not liked to be called a medium.

This book has helped me to recognize that there is no need to have titles in order to be an awakened spirit, or to be a vessel of service of the Divine and for humanity. And yet, ironically, this entire book is dedicated to learning how to become a *Master!* What I have learned and wish to impart on you is that *Mastery* is not a title but an essence that we become as we allow ourselves to become unified with our natural state of Spirit and with the God Force.

When we are able to wake up in the morning and realize that we are no longer harboring extreme heavy emotions, dreading on the problems of the world, but using our spiritual resources to send healing energy, when we can stand in front of the mirror and say, "I love you" and really, really mean it, and when we can accept that life is always going to be "happening" but that we do not have to be affected by it, then, we can joyfully acknowledge that we have become Masters of our expression and an essence of the God/Goddess. *The Attributes of Mastery* have become you... Amen! It has been an amazing joy and honor to write this book and to share my deepest moments of life with you. I hope that you are inspired and motivated to spark your own, unique light and mastery to the world.

About The Author

For the first time since beginning her writing career, Blanca has intimately written and shared parts of her life that created the foundation for her spirituality and mastery.

Her endeavor is to inspire you to recognize that mastery in not about perfection but about the passion to be the very best than you can be.

"I truly believe that the Attributes presented in this book can truly change our lives and assist us in reaching a state of self-realization and spiritual bliss."

If you were inspired by this book, help to promote it by recommending it to others.

You can learn more about Blanca's books and practice by visiting her website at: http://blancabeyar.org

AYNI
BOOKS

"Ayni" is a Quechua word meaning "reciprocity" – sharing,
giving and receiving - whatever you give out comes back to you.
To be in Ayni is to be in balance, harmony and right relationship
with oneself and nature, of which we are all an intrinsic part.
Complementary and Alternative approaches to health and
well-being essentially follow a holistic model, within which one
is given support and encouragement to move towards a state of
balance, true health and wholeness, ultimately leading to
the awareness of one's unique place in the Universal jigsaw
of life – Ayni, in fact.